BRIGHT IDEAS

Inspirations for ENGLISH

Published by Scholastic
Publications Ltd,
Villiers House,
Clarendon Avenue,
Leamington Spa,
Warwickshire CV32 5PR

© 1991 Scholastic Publications
Ltd

Reprinted 1992, 1993

Written by Helen Hadley
Edited by Juliet Gladston
Sub-edited by Catherine Baker
Designed by Sue Limb
Series designed by Juanita
Puddifoot
Illustrated by Francis Scappaticci
Cover artwork by Connie Jude

Designed using Aldus
Pagemaker
Processed by Pages Bureau,
Leamington Spa
Artwork by Liz Preece, Castle
Graphics, Kenilworth
Printed by Ebenezer Baylis &
Son, Worcester

**British Library Cataloguing in
Publication Data**
Hadley, Helen
  English. - (Inspirations).
  1. English language
  I. Title Ii. Series
  420

  ISBN 0-590-76404-7

CONTENTS

INTRODUCTION

English

Language is a life skill; it is through language that we explore, organise and make sense of our experiences and develop skills essential in the adult world. The learning of language and its uses is a process that goes on for the whole of our lives.

At one time, in the teaching of English, the end product was all; children were expected to speak, read and write perfectly all the time. Next, stimulus was the focus. Now we are concerned with the process, and the ways in which children become proficient language users.

Language is a means by which messages are sent and received. The clearer and more appropriate the communication, the more effectively the message is passed on.

We want children to be able to communicate clearly to a variety of audiences, across a range of purposes, in both oral and written language modes. We need to extend the breadth of their language use, their competence and their enjoyment in using oral and written language. We need to catch their enthusiasm, engage their curiosity and use it to develop their understanding of language, so that they will not drop their skills on leaving school. But at all times we must make sure that the learning steps are small, and that the gap between knowledge and strategies is not so great that learning cannot occur.

Children need good models to work from. For spoken language, they will find examples in our various uses of it and the way we speak to others. They need to hear high-quality stories read with clear enunciation and variety of tone and voice. Our writing both for and with children must be in the style we want them to copy. These forms of modelling all add to the child's understanding of language and her ability to make it work for her.

BACKGROUND

How to use this book

This book covers many different aspects of English, and includes suggestions for topic work and assessment. Photocopiable material is provided to support the text where appropriate.

The introduction to each chapter points to some important aspects for consideration. This section is followed by practical ideas for stimulating language developments, which are concerned with both content and process. All the tasks are designed to have meaning and purpose for the child.

Each activity gives an indication of the optimum size of group for the task and the age range for which it is intended, but these are only guidelines. Choose from them to suit the needs of your children and your planned programme of work.

Speaking and listening

In some ways oral language is easier than written language, but it can also be more difficult. Listening to a story or talking with friends is relaxing, but it is much harder to listen attentively in order to answer questions or remember details, or to prepare and give a talk in front of others.

The first chapter of this book gives suggestions for developing children's oral language skills individually, in groups or in front of a wider audience.

Reading

Firstly, we want children to enjoy reading. We want them to be grabbed by what they read, to thrust books under each other's noses, saying 'You want to read this book – it's brilliant!' To be able to do this they need to acquire knowledge about reading.

Children need to understand the different ways in which meaning can be conveyed, and how texts can be layered like onions, so that multiple levels of meaning can be extracted by the reader.

Children also need to know and understand the conventions for relaying meaning. Daily, it seems, new technologies increase the variety of methods, forms and contexts by which communication is transmitted. Children need to work confidently in these media so that they can use them to good effect.

In order to become good readers, children need to learn to interpret a variety of cues which they can call upon when they get stuck. Various ways are suggested in Chapter 2 to help children develop as readers.

Writing

Writing begins with scribble, and in time it can grow into a medium for communication across a wide range of purposes and to a variety of audiences. To be effective, a writer needs to be able to use the genre appropriate to what she wishes to convey.

Chapter 3 on writing concentrates more on process than on product, encouraging the development of a number of different ways of working with fiction and non-fiction. Suggestions are also included for redrafting writing, through self-monitoring and teacher intervention.

Spelling

A writer who can spell is able to write down what he wants to say without the anxiety of wondering whether it can be read by others.

In Chapter 4 there are suggestions for how to teach children to spell, and ways of encourage spelling through games and word play.

Handwriting

An ability to get down what you want to say quickly and easily, without having to give thought to letter formation, frees a writer to concentrate on what she wishes to communicate.

Process is stressed in this book, but good content can be improved and made more persuasive by the quality of its presentation. Therefore, we need to encourage children to develop an easy, relaxed and legible writing style. They also need to acquire techniques for presenting their work in a different and exciting way.

Chapter 5 suggests ways of achieving these aims in the classroom, and the writing style suggested is one often used in primary schools.

Cross-curricular ideas

Chapter 6 considers ways of linking work in English with ideas relevant to many other subjects in the curriculum.

Almost any subject can be used as a basis for topic work. This chapter looks at English as a starting point for topics, giving suggestions to show how stories, poems and sayings can act as the stimulus for a wide range of work covering many areas of the curriculum.

English through topic work

Children need a wide variety of stimuli for their language work, and the opportunity to use and encounter language in a variety of different and interesting contexts. Once children have had this experience, they will be free to use language at will. They will then be in control of the language they use, rather than being limited by it.

Topic work provides opportunities for children to speak, read, write and experiment with language in different forms through a wide range of activities. This chapter concentrates on the place of English in topic work, suggesting a number of themes and developing the English strands of those themes.

Assessment and record keeping

Chapter 8 considers the use of assessment and its place in planning and structuring our programmes of work, in evaluation and self-monitoring. Suggestions for possible methods of record keeping are also given, along with charts to show stages of development through the primary years.

Photocopiable pages

Some of the photocopiable pages provided here are generic; others relate to particular activities. They all link with different aspects of English, including topic work, assessment and record keeping. The pages range in style from proformas, which you can complete in whichever way best suits the needs of your class, to straightforward activity sheets which you can photocopy for the children's use. You are free to photocopy and adapt all the sheets for your own requirements.

Bibliography

This section contains a list of useful and interesting books to support teaching in all the areas covered in this book.

Attainment targets

This chart indicates the National Curriculum levels that could be covered, within one or more attainment targets, by each activity.

In conclusion, this book is not a complete curriculum in itself, but a collection of ideas and suggestions, looking at the involvement of English across the curriculum. It is meant to be an aid, to add to and extend the work you are already doing to help children become confident users of English.

CHAPTER 1

Speaking and listening

In some ways spoken language is easier for children to use than written language, because the labour of writing things down is removed. But in other ways it is harder. Writing is a private task; if mistakes are made, then the paper can be screwed up and thrown away and no one need be any the wiser. However, speech is a public task. Errors are voiced with little chance of redress and, worse still, a listener can mock or scoff at the speaker's ineptitudes or obvious mistakes. Therefore, it is essential that you establish the right atmosphere in which to encourage talk. This atmosphere should be one in which the children:

• feel secure;
• feel free to explore new ideas;
• know that what they say and how they say it is respected;
• know that their attempts to express their own thoughts, ideas and feelings clearly, succinctly and confidently are encouraged.

BACKGROUND

Children need to experience a diversity of oral language situations in order to develop their speaking and listening skills. The best situations are those where there is a wide variety of different things to talk about, where there are real opportunities for using language and where the children can use talk to increase their understanding of the world around them.

However, it is important not to neglect the use of social language – greeting people, thanking them, enquiring and complaining. Children need to learn to interact with other people. This involves:
• observing reactions;
• interpreting reactions;
• listening to responses;

• matching responses and style;
• redressing wrong impressions;
• voicing opposing opinions courteously;
• taking turns.

It can be seen from this list that listening forms an integral part of talking. Listening is an active process involving the listener in selecting, making judgements and using information to make predictions. It is important to remember this, as it will help when providing opportunities for active listening.

Children should not only listen to what someone else is saying; they need to listen to themselves as well. They need time to pause, reflect and review. What did they learn? How well did they do the task?

Not all learning situations require talk. In our desire to release children from the strait-jacket of being forbidden

to talk, we must not be guilty of requiring every word spoken to be 'on-task'. 'On-task' talk is not always needed to complete a task. Low-level tasks, such as colouring a picture or painting a model, are often achieved just as well while talking about something entirely different. While talking in these situations, children will still be honing their interactive skills and refining the social context of language usage.

Not all activities need discussion; some tasks are better done in communion with one's own thoughts. But situations that require everyone to participate in sharing ideas and making decisions lead to 'on-task' talk, and the task itself will determine whether the talk is practical, exploratory or imaginative.

Talk is central to all teaching. If it is to be developed profitably, it must be structured and planned to assist learning and develop oral skills. This chapter looks at some ways of developing oral language which may help you to develop real situations for talk in your classroom.

ACTIVITIES

1. Memory

Age range
All ages.

Group size
Whole class or small groups (the younger the children, the smaller the group).

What you need
No special requirements.

What to do
Explain to the children that you are all going to help make a list. Begin by saying 'At the supermarket I bought...' or 'In my Christmas stocking I had...' and name one item. Then ask the first child to repeat what you have said and add another item of her own. The next child then repeats it all and adds his item, and so on. Make sure that you yourself begin and end the list.

Encourage the children to use nouns and adjectives creatively when giving items for the lists. Only the youngest children should use nouns alone. Over time, the children will become very imaginative in their use of language.

Variations of the game could include:
• In my lunch box I had...
• At the zoo I saw...
• For my birthday I had...
• With my pocket money I bought...

2. Listening to music

Age range
All ages.

Group size
Whole class or small groups.

What you need
Tape recorder, tapes of descriptive or mood music.

What to do
Children should be encouraged to be active rather than passive listeners, and to learn to listen for a clear purpose.

Tape a track of music that invokes feelings or pictures in the mind, such as the elephant track from *Carnival of the Animals* or *Danse Macabre* (by Saint-Saëns), 'The Sugar Plum Fairy' from *The Nutcracker Suite* by Tchaikovsky, or *The Sorcerer's Apprentice* by Dukas.

First, let the children listen to the music with their eyes closed. Ask them to try to imagine the scene. Then ask them to listen two or three times more with their eyes open. After having heard the music a few times the children can then discuss what the music suggests, either as a class or in groups. Ask them to give reasons for their conclusions. A movement or drama lesson could develop from here.

3. Blind man's buff

Age range
All ages.

Group size
Any number.

What you need
A blindfold, various large objects such as a chair, waste-paper basket, etc.

What to do
Before beginning the game, let the children get used to being blindfolded. Ask them to go for a walk around the school in

pairs with one of the children in the pair blindfolded. The other child should instruct the blindfolded child how to negotiate the route successfully.

Once back in the classroom, divide the class into four teams and send one team to a neighbouring classroom (with that teacher's agreement). Then you can push back the tables to leave a wide walk-way, and strew it with objects such as chairs, some upright and some turned over, a waste-paper basket, a book, a school bag, and so on. The size and arrangement of the objects should be changed for each game.

Next blindfold one child in the exiled group and lead him back to the classroom, where a member of an opposing team should try to talk him along the walk-way so that he does not touch anything. The 'talker' starts with ten points but loses a point every time her charge touches something.

Each team can enter four players for the event, two as talkers and two as blindfolded walkers, and over several days each has a turn. The winning team is the one which has accumulated the most points at the end of the series.

Further activity
A discussion about how it felt to negotiate the obstacles blindfolded gives deeper insight into being blind.

4. Prediction: 1

Age range
Six to eleven.
Group size
Whole class or small groups.
What you need
A good short story, paper and pencils.
What to do
Read aloud a suitable short story, one stage at a time. At intervals, stop and ask the children to predict what will happen next. They should use active listening and deductive skills to help them answer.

Together, write four or five different ways in which the story could move forward, and measure these against the author's concept.

Discuss whether there was another path or course of action open to the author, and the effect this would have had upon the story.

5. Prediction: 2

Age range
All ages.
Group size
Whole class.
What you need
A good short story, paper and pencils.
What to do
Divide the short story into approximately four parts and write a few questions about each part which are to be discussed at the end of each section.

Divide the children into groups of five or six, and give each group a copy of the parts. Each group should elect a leader, who hands out the sections one page at a time as and when they are required.

Ask the groups to read the first part of the story and discuss what could happen next. When they have come to a decision, the group leader should give out the next part. At the end of this part, they can discuss whether their predictions were correct or, if not, why not. They should then discuss what could happen next, moving on to the next part, and so on.

6. Talk about

Age range
All ages.
Group size
Individuals or pairs.
What you need
A set of blank cards, a timer, a selection of magazines.
What to do
Prepare the blank cards by

sticking pictures from magazines, drawing pictures or writing subjects on them. Spread the cards out face down on a table. Ask one child to choose a card and turn it over. The child must now describe what is on the card without naming the object, or talk on the specified subject for a set length of time – 30 seconds or a minute. The timer should be started as soon as the child is ready to speak, but you should not allow more than a minute for thinking time.

Further activity
Ask the children in turn to explain to the rest of the class how they made a model, constructed a net for a cuboid, or conducted an experiment.

7. I remember when

Age range
All ages.
Group size
Whole class or small groups.
What you need
No special requirements.
What to do
Tell an anecdote about something that happened when you were a child. 'I remember when I was little I...', 'My big sister used to...' or 'When I was little my Gran used to...'. Talk about serious things as well as humorous ones. Let the children ask you questions about it, and respond openly. Then ask them to think about something that happened to them when they were younger and encourage them to talk about it, sharing their experiences with others. The others will often respond with 'Yes, that happened to me...' and so the discussion takes off.

This kind of talk helps children to realise that while they are all different, in many ways they are the same; the same sorts of things happen and the same kinds of feelings come to the surface. They learn that they need not be ashamed of certain things, and that it is how they handle situations that matters. They also learn to look objectively at themselves and to assess their responses, asking questions such as 'Would it be the same now? If not, why not?'

8. Picture stories

Age range
All ages.
Group size
Whole class or small groups.
What you need
A series of four or five pictures to tell a story. The concepts must be suitable for the children's age and ability.
What to do
Picture stories provide a variety of different opportunities for talk. Children can build a coherent story with a beginning, a middle and an end; they can focus on details, examine cause and effect, and go beyond what is there, imagining elements of the story which are not visible.

Initially, show the children the pictures one at a time, in the order of the story, so that they know the sequence. Once they understand the idea, show the pictures in a random sequence – you may even end up with a totally different story!

Ask questions about each picture, such as 'What is happening in the picture?' 'What happened before?' 'What could happen next?' 'Why do you think that?' This last question is important because it helps children to analyse and rationalise their thinking. An understanding of the ways they obtain and use cues will help them to look more closely at the world around them and make more sense of it.

Show one picture and ask some questions about it. After a number of responses, show another picture and ask some more questions. Then ask, 'Did this happen before or after the last picture?' 'What makes you think that?' Continue this process for the remaining cards, until the story ends.

9. People stories

Age range
All ages.
Group size
Small groups or whole class.
What you need
A flannel-graph or similar, characters cut from books or magazines or drawn, backed with flannel or velcro, 'props' – real or pictures.
What to do
Encourage the children to tell a story and to enact it by moving the cut-out characters about on a flannel-graph. Let them select two characters and one 'prop', and build the story around them.

In case you or the children get stuck, have in reserve some short 'starters' for each section of the story, in the style of the consequences game, to prompt ideas. For example:

'X
met Y
in a Z...
X said to Y...
Y replied...
So they...
After a while...
X wanted...
But Y...
X said...
But Y said...
So X...
and Y...
Later on...
So they...'

It may help if you start this oral story-telling by using characters the children know; then they will have ideas about how the characters should behave. You can also use this idea to create original stories.

10. Talking about our senses

Age range
Five to seven.
Group size
Small groups.
What you need
Large sheets of paper, pencils, crayons or paints.
What to do
The more acutely our senses are developed, the more we take in about the world. This in turn gives us more to think, talk and write about. The earlier we encourage children to use their senses, the richer their language will be. This activitity links with the one on writing about the senses in Chapter 3 (Activity 16, pages 46 and 47).

Explore each of the senses with the children, and write on a large sheet of paper a sentence from what each child has said. Pin up the sentences at the children's eye level, so that they can read them with you and go on to read them for themselves. Let them draw pictures which relate to the different senses, and use these together with the sentences to make booklets. These can be borrowed as take-home books.

In this activity the emphasis is on the teacher writing down what the children say, but older infants can write for themselves about what they have seen, heard, touched, tasted and smelled. Here are some suggestions to help stimulate work on the senses.
Sight
Take the children out into the playground. What can they see? Ask them to focus on what they see rather than what they hear.

On returning to the classroom, ask the children to tell you all the things they can remember seeing. With a little judicious prompting you can encourage them to tell you more than merely 'I saw an aeroplane'. Ask them to give the object's colour, shape or size and say what it was doing. Then you can write it up for them.

I saw two girls skipping

A small bird flew into the big tree

I saw Sally and Jane laughing.

feely bag

Other 'sights' can be found in the classroom, entrance hall, street, down the lane or in a park or field.

Sound

Talk about words that describe sounds, and list the ones which the children suggest.

Ask them to close their eyes and focus on the sounds around them. You can do this in the classroom, or in other suitable locations like the playground or the street, and you can also use taped sounds.

Ask the children to talk about the sounds that they heard, and to describe them. Write up the sentences they dictate on a large sheet of paper; for example, 'In the street I can hear cars racing by, two ladies talking, a dog barking ...'. You can then look at sounds in familiar scenes; for example, 'In my kitchen', 'In my living room', 'In the bath'.

Touch

Talk about words that describe the texture of different materials and substances. Ask the children to bring in different objects that are interesting to touch, and display them on a touch table. Put single items in a 'feely bag' and ask the children to describe the feel of the items.

Then you can go out with the children into the playground and touch the walls, trees, windows, wooden fences, grass, leaves, railings, and so on.

When you return, discuss what the children have touched and write up their comments. Encourage them to say more than 'The wall is rough', and see whether they can say things like 'The wall feels like rough sandpaper'.

Taste

Begin by talking with the children about which foods they like and dislike. What do they have for different meals? What are their favourite meals?

Take in some potato crisps, small seedless grapes, cubes of bread, carrot matchsticks, and Smarties or jelly babies. Ask the children to take one type of food at a time, and hold it in their mouths as long as they can, so that they can concentrate while they are eating it. What is the flavour they taste on their tongue? How does it feel? What happens as they eat it? Does it have to be sucked or chewed, or do they have to do both?

Ask the children to make up sentences which describe what happens each time, and write them up for them.

NB It is important to find out first whether any of the children have any food allergies.

Smell

Care has to be taken when encouraging children to smell things. Some teachers may prefer to avoid the subject altogether, but talking about the dangers of smelling noxious substances can form an important part of a discussion about smell.

The sense of smell is closely linked with that of taste but, of all the senses, it is the hardest for young children to describe. Bring in a selection of items, such as an orange, an empty perfume bottle, some roses, some blackberries and a lemon, and ask the children to smell each in turn. You can then talk about words that describe smells. Encourage the children to talk about their favourite smells, and ask them to make up a sentence about them.

11. Listening to stories

Age range
Five to nine.
Group size
The whole class.
What you need
A good story.
What to do
Choose a good story to read aloud to the children, and decide what you would like them to gain from it. Design some questions to ask at the end of the story to bring out these features in particular, rather than ranging through the whole story.

Before you start reading, tell the children that you want them to listen carefully because you are going to ask them about a specific aspect of the story afterwards. You might be doing a topic on homes and houses, and choose to read the 'Three Little Pigs'. Your questions would then be on houses, for example:
• Is straw a good material to use to build a house?
• Are sticks a good material to use to build a house?
• Are bricks good for house building?
• Why did the wolf go to the house of straw first?
• Why do you think the wolf left the house of bricks till last? Was he right?

Of course, not all stories need to be treated in this way, but if you are linking them to a project then that link could be made explicit.

12. Show and tell

Age range
Five to nine.
Group size
The whole class.
What you need
A display table.
What to do
At the beginning of the year, tell the children that each day three of them will be invited to bring something to school to talk about. For the rest of that day the objects remain on display for others to see. Ask them to make sure that they are allowed to bring the item of interest to school, and tell them that you want them to find out as much as they can about it before bringing it in.

At show and tell time, rather than having fairly low-level chat, each child has a turn to talk in depth about something real that holds meaning for them. New words are introduced to the children's vocabulary and the speaker can be asked what certain subject-specific words mean.

The children soon become used to this practice and grow more expert at talking in front of others, stating their views and sharing what they have learned. Work of this sort is based on the principle that 'he who teaches learns'.

Keep a list so that all the children have the opportunity to bring something in. Even a reluctant talker will be persuaded by gentle leading and a little help.

13. What is it?

Age range
Six to eleven.
Group size
Whole class.
What you need
A three-sided barricade, a variety of small objects such as a cup, a toy car, a book, a pencil case etc.
What to do
Set out a number of small objects behind the barricade or screen so that the children

cannot see what they are. They can then take it in turns to stand behind the barricade and describe one of the items without calling it by its proper name. They should talk about its size, colour, how it is used, and so on.

The child who guesses the correct name may choose whether or not he wants to be the next 'talker'. It is important that children are not stopped from making guesses because they don't want to be the next one up at the front. Plenty of children will want to, and the others will come to it in their own time, especially if they are encouraged to participate in other activities on listening and speaking.

Further activity
You can vary the game by asking the children to question the child at the front, who is only allowed to make one statement at a time. This gives minimal clues and requires the questioners to hold details in their short-term memory.

Another version only allows the child being questioned to nod or shake his head. This means that the other children can ask only those questions that can be answered by yes or no.

14. Talk to a theme

Age range
Seven to eleven.
Group size
Whole class or small groups.
What you need
Blank cards, envelope or small bag. An overhead projector may be helpful.
What to do
Write out the names of various objects on separate pieces of card, and place them in an envelope or small bag. Choose items which are suited to the age and experiences of the children, such as a clock, a digital watch, a tape or video recorder, a vacuum cleaner, a bicycle, a torch, a flower, a bird, a board game. Small groups of two or three children can select a card and then prepare a talk on the subject shown. They must research all the technical words so that

they can use precise terminology when giving their talk. They can also write on a transparency a list of the words they will use which may be unfamiliar.

By learning to use the correct words, mistakes are avoided and less time is spent in explanation. The children's vocabulary is broadened while they learn to speak, with confidence, from a basis of knowledge.

15. Happenings

Age range
Seven to eleven.
Group size
Individuals, pairs or small groups.
What you need
Blank cards about 75 × 125cm, pencils.
What to do
Ask the children to think about the most important things that have happened to them. These things can be exciting, happy, sad, unusual, different, good or bad. After about five minutes, ask them to list up to three things which they would like to talk about.

In pairs or groups, they can then take turns to talk about one of the events, describing what happened, how they felt and how it ended.

The children can plan their talks by noting the three or four stages of the event on separate cards. For example:
• going to the swimming pool,
• scared to go down the chute,
• persuaded into having a go,
• how they felt.
They can then use these cards to talk from.

The cards can also be used to make a rough draft of the speech, which can then be redrafted (see Activity 30, page 54). After planning the presentation of the piece in terms of its title, the illustrations and the layout of text, the children can write up their work 'in best'.

The collected works can be mounted in a book, perhaps entitled 'It Happened to Me', or 'The Time of My Life', and used as part of a theme display or as a focus for the class assembly.
Further activity
Ask the children to choose another event from their lists to tell to the class or write about.

16. Puppets

Age range
Seven to eleven.
Group size
Small groups.
What you need
Puppets and props made from junk material.
What to do
In small groups the children can decide on the type of story they want to use puppets to tell. They should discuss what the puppets will look like, what kinds of characters the puppets will have and what they will wear.

They can then plot the story and decide on the other things they will need, such as the stage, the back-cloth, the props and the lighting. Then they can set to work to make them.

Puppets can be made out of paper bags, or paper plates on sticks; they don't need to be elaborate, merely functional. The purpose of the task is to engender different forms of talk – discussion, collaboration, listening to the views of others, planning, plotting and play-acting.

17. Mind words

Age range
Seven to eleven.
Group size
Small groups.
What you need
A small pot and some tokens.
What to do
'Mind words' is a game that requires concentration and encourages children to search their minds for word patterns.

The idea of this game is to build up words, letter by letter. The first player, with a word in mind, says the first letter of that word; for example, 'c' for 'coach'. The second player adds the letter 'o', perhaps thinking of the word 'corn'. The next player then thinks of the word 'coal' and therefore adds the letter 'a'.

If one player thinks that a letter will not help to build a real word, she can challenge it. For instance, if the fourth player adds the letter 'c', the next player could challenge this, claiming that there is no word beginning 'coac'. The fourth player, however, can refute the challenge with the word 'coach'.

The challenger is then fined one token. The successful player earns one token for winning the challenge and one for finishing the word.

If a player cannot go he puts a token into the pot. The pot is won by the player who completes the word.

18. Frog hopping

Age range
Seven to eleven.
Group size
Six to ten.
What you need
One chair per child, alphabet cards for children to wear.
What to do
Ask each group to set their chairs in a semicircle or horseshoe to allow for discussion. The children can then sit on the chairs and label themselves from left to right with the alphabet cards.

The object of the game is for two or more children to change places making as few moves as possible; for example, simple moves like A and F to change places, or more complicated ones like reversing the order, or a three-way exchange. The children are only allowed to move by exchanging places with the person next to them or by leap-frogging over one person.

Each move and the succeeding ones have to be discussed and reasoned by the whole group. It is fascinating listening to the level of reasoning and debate that comes from this task. You can watch for children who are not participating orally, you can see who argues the case logically, you can draw out a point if it hovers on the edge of being sound, you can watch the change of group dynamics. Most important of all, you can stand back, listen, and make assessments about the children's oral development.

Further activity
If each group is set the same task, the element of competition gives a new dimension to the task.

19. Constructive criticism

Age range
Seven to eleven.
Group size
The whole class or small groups.
What you need
Pieces of their own work selected by the children.
What to do
One child in each small group can read out her piece of work. The others should listen

and tell her whether there were any gaps or inconsistencies. 'I don't get what happened when...' or 'You left Fred in the attic and the next time he was in the kitchen. How did he get there?' 'What does such-and-such a word mean?' 'I thought Sadie was his sister, but then you said she was his friend', or 'He was skinny enough to get through the window, then he was out of breath because he was too fat. Which is right?'

Questions of this sort mean the critic has really had to listen in order to ask useful and searching questions. As with all new ways of working, it takes time to develop the skill of criticising constructively, but it is well worth the effort.

20. Heads and tails

Age range
Eight to eleven.
Group size
Small groups.
What you need
No special requirements.
What to do
Ask the group to decide on a category, such as food, animals, machines, towns, books, television programmes or plants. The first player says the name of something in the category – for example, tomato, in the category of plants. The next has to think of something beginning with the last letter of that word, such as 'onion'. The next player follows with another item in the same category; for example, 'nettle'.

If a word is repeated, that player drops out and the game continues until there is only one child left.

21. Argue your case

Age range
Nine to eleven.
Group size
The whole class.
What you need
No special requirements.
What to do
Ask the children to suggest a suitable topic for debate. They will suggest topics that matter to them and have a meaningful context. Select one which is likely to raise the most issues. Discuss the topic with the class, and then agree the motion to be argued; for example, 'The best cooks are men'; 'People with red hair have bad tempers'; 'Do good manners matter?'; 'Fear of punishment makes people behave'; 'Who is really free?'; 'Does it matter how you look?'.

When the motion is agreed, each child can research it and discuss it at home. The children should then write lists of all the points they want to make in support of their views.

After a few days the children can divide into groups strongly for or against the motion, and each group should elect three spokespersons to argue their case. A date can then be set for the debate.

On the appointed day, set up a lectern and ask one of the children speaking for the motion to start. The sides then take turns to state their views. If any view expressed is on a child's list, it can be ticked off.

After the main speakers have argued their case, any other points not previously raised can be made.

The class teacher is arbiter and, after listing the main issues raised, declares the result.

22. Interviews

Age range
Nine to eleven.
Group size
Individuals or pairs.
What you need
Tape recorders (not essential).
What to do
Interviews often form part of project work, but if they are to be worthwhile, an interview plan should be made. First the interviewer must decide what he would like to know and devise questions which would solicit that information. Next he must write or talk to the person to be interviewed and ask if they are prepared to be interviewed. Plenty of time should be allowed for the interview because many people, especially old people, do like to talk. Responses can be noted on paper or taped.

The notes or tape recording can be used to make a draft from which the final pen portrait can be written. A photograph of the interviewee adds considerably to the finished product.

NB It is a courtesy to show the finished copy to the person who kindly consented to be interviewed.

23. Media criticism

Age range
Nine to eleven.
Group size
The whole class or small groups.
What you need
Videos, books, newspapers.
What to do
Children should be encouraged to look critically at the world around them, and not to accept something just because it is there. We want them to make objective judgements, not value-laden ones.

Video an advertisement and let the children view it three or four times straight through. Then freeze-frame it at scene changes and discuss what has happened up to that point. What is the advertiser doing? How is he achieving it? What subtleties is he employing to persuade the viewer?

If a video is not available, use advertisements in colour magazines or newspapers. This technique can be used for all kinds of communication, including the children's writing, the mass media, books, articles, poems, diagrams, shows, talks and any other form of presentation.

Ask questions like:
• Does it do what it sets out to do?
• Is it fact or opinion?
• Is it biased or prejudiced in any way?
• Does the premise hold?
• Does it make sense?
• Is it successful?
• Does it gain your sympathy?

As children develop critical awareness of the writing of others, their own writing will become more effective.

CHAPTER 2

Reading

Being able to read is just about the most important thing we ever learn to do.

In this world many things happen which we cannot experience first-hand but which have a direct effect upon our lives. We have to rely upon written accounts in the press for information, and it is upon our reading of these accounts that we base our opinions and make our judgements. Reading can help us to answer questions, resolve problems or research topics in greater depth. Reading is also the means by which we can withdraw from the world, escape its insistent demands and retire into a private place to restore and refresh our minds.

If we cannot read, virtually all these options are closed to us. Those who cannot read are embarrassed in our literate society and employ all sorts of subterfuge to disguise the fact. Awareness of inability to read brings negative feelings in its wake, leading to poor attitudes to learning and a lowering of self-esteem even in children as young as six years of age.

BACKGROUND

But what is reading?

It is the means by which we derive meaning from text. It is a two-way conversation between the writer and the reader, the one leading the other into a wider world of experience.

Some children seem to learn to read with very little help, if they simply have access to a selection of lively, interesting books. Others will only come to reading after a great deal of slow, painstaking effort from themselves, their parents and their teachers. Most children fall between these two extremes.

We need to provide a lively and exciting reading environment where children want to learn to read, supported by a clear and structured reading philosophy. We need to encourage children to become active listeners to stories and poems, to become reflective in their reading and to develop positive attitudes towards reading and books generally.

We want children to share books, to enjoy stories and talk about them from an early age. We want them to develop into confident, independent readers, using the full range of phonic, idiomatic, grammatical and contextual clues to interpret text. Children also need to read a range of material in appropriate ways, skimming, scanning and reading closely, as the need demands.

Children should not read merely for the sake of reading, but for a purpose – for interest, for information or to escape into a private world opened to them by a skilled writer.

Choosing fiction books

Children need real and compelling books if they are to catch the reading bug. Most children, whatever their age, like realistic stories about characters of a similar age to themselves, who do things that the children do themselves, or that they would like to do. In identifying with the characters and plot, children more readily make sense of the story.

The same factors apply to books which you read aloud to children, although when reading aloud it is generally best to choose books which are more difficult than the children could read for themselves, in order to lead them forward in exploring the language and structure of stories.

Books for children need to have the kind of jacket that attracts the would-be reader, page layouts that appeal, type that is not too small and a title that beckons.

If you are choosing books for beginning readers, there are some fabulous picture books available. Some caption books too tell great stories; you just have to be selective.

For top infants or lower juniors, the magic of fairy and folk tales has a strong grip, and children enjoy stories of princelings and paupers, of witches and innocents. Many children will also be ready for short novels, which give them a chance to get thoroughly 'stuck into a book'.

Later on in the primary school, children will enjoy a range of books including realistic stories, animal tales, myths and legends, stories from different cultures, adventure stories (past and present), humour and fantasy.

Children need to be encouraged to read voraciously and widely. They will probably also read 'rubbish' from time to time. However, we must be careful not to put down what children may be enjoying – at least they are reading something!

Our task is to lead children to realise that they get much more enjoyment and value from a good book. One of the best ways to do this is to be sure that the books we provide can capture the child's interest and make him want to go on reading.

Choosing non-fiction books

Criteria for choosing non-fiction books change as children get older, but certain features are constant.

• Is the jacket attractive? Does it give the researcher clues about its contents?

• Is the layout clear and easy to follow, or is the text so fragmented that it is easy to lose the sense of what is written?

• Is the information authentic and up to date? Is it written in an interesting, readable style?

• Are the illustrations closely related to the text? Do they complement the text, or are they just decorations?

• How is the book organised? Does it have numbered pages, a contents list, an index, a bibliography and a range of open-ended ideas for further work?

Choose books by examining them for these criteria. It is better to go on searching than to make do with books that turn children off the fascination of finding out.

Choosing books is not easy, and it takes time. You need to see a book to know whether it is right for the children in your class, but it is worth making the effort to do this. Books are expensive; they need to be right.

Organising your books

Fiction

For five- to seven-year-olds, do not sort fiction into levels of difficulty, but allow the children the freedom to choose the books that interest them. A child may not be able to read the text of a book but will often spend a long time studying the pictures, or may be able to read a difficult book that interests her with much more ease than a simpler book that she finds uninteresting.

When new books come in, set up a display of them, talk about them and read them at story time.

For older children, develop a school policy for colour-coding books into categories such as animals, adventure, mystery, fantasy or sci-fi. If some books seem to fit into more than one category, ask a child who has read the book to say where the strongest emphasis lies. If you cannot agree, put the book in a general fiction category.

If you sort the books in each category alphabetically by author, children can quickly find their favourites. Teach them the 'five-finger test' (see Activity 16, page 34), and then the task of finding an interesting book they can read becomes even easier.

Non-fiction

Colour code your information books according to curriculum areas, using colours to create links, but do have a consistent policy throughout the school. If books cross curriculum boundaries, use a broad strip of colour to show the main subject matter, with a narrow strip of another colour as a cross-reference.

Setting up a new system is time-consuming, but once it is established new books which come in will easily be slotted into the system.

ACTIVITIES

1. Sustained silent reading (SSR)

Age range
All ages.
Group size
Whole class.
What you need
A good story.
What to do
Begin each afternoon with the whole class reading silently for about 15 minutes.

Books should be chosen before the children go to lunch, so that as soon as they come into the classroom they can settle down to some silent reading. You should also read silently.

The stories must be fiction, and the children should have a chance to really get into their story without noise and disturbance around them. Make a rule that they are not allowed to move about the classroom, to get up or to change their books during this period.

Have a reporting session after SSR once a week, so you can all discuss the books you have been reading that week and share your enthusiasm for them.

Encourage parents to join with their children and do the same at home every night.

Working together in SSR in this way, the children's reading and their enjoyment of it will increase dramatically.

2. Early reading books

Age range
Five to six.
Group size
Individuals.
What you need
Attractive one- or two-lined caption books.

What to do
Ask a child to choose a book he has not read before from the shelf of caption books. Then sit beside him and talk together about the story and what happens on each page using the words of the caption wherever possible. Talk about difficult words or names. It is important that children know all about the book they are going to read before they read it, as they will then find the process of reading a lot easier.

Start by letting the child read the book, helping him with words he finds difficult, occasionally reading the text with him. Then read the book a second time together. Read the text at normal speed, pulling

the child along with you, so that he develops a sense of what it is like to read with fluency. This way the child is not asked to 'perform' every time he reads; anxiety can force errors. He will rather feel that you are performing the act of reading with him.

3. Picture story

Age range
Five to six.
Group size
Individuals or pairs.
What you need
A series of pictures from magazines or books, card, adhesive, shoe boxes, envelopes, contact film.
What to do
Cut out a series of about five pictures which tell a story, from magazines or old books. There should be one beginning picture, three event pictures and a conclusion picture. Alternatively, you

could draw the pictures, or use photographs. Mount the pictures separately on card and cover them, if necessary, with transparent contact film. Place them in a trimmed used envelope or a plastic wallet and store them upright in a shoe box or similar container. It is a good idea to make a number of these stories over time, as they will last for a long time.

The children can spread out the series of cards and arrange them in the order which they think tells the story. Ask them to tell you what happens at the beginning of the story, what happens next and why, and then how the story ends. Ask them questions about the story, and get them to reason cause and effect.

4. Same as...

Age range
Five to six.
Group size
Individuals or pairs.
What you need
A tray or box with pairs of objects, or pictures of objects on separate cards.

What to do
Using picture cards or real objects, the children can play any or all of the following games.
Game one
Place a number of pairs of real objects or pictures on a tray or in a box. Make sure that some of the things are different from each other and some quite similar. The children can then sort the objects into pairs.
Game two
Sort the pairs of objects or pictures into two piles, and place one pile behind each player. The players then take it in turn to call 'Go!' On hearing the call, each child should pull out one object or card from behind them. If the objects are the same, they should call 'Snap!' and the first person to do so wins the pair. Play until all the objects have been paired; the winner is the one with the most pairs.
Game three
Select a variety of objects, most of which begin with the same letter. Older or more advanced children can use pictures of the objects instead.

Place two cards on the table, one with the initial letter of most of the objects on it, and another with the same letter crossed through in another colour. The children should

then sort the objects into two sets, those that begin with the letter and those that do not.
Game four
Use cards, and sort them into two piles. The players should have a pile each and place them face down on the table. They then turn up a card at the same time, and if the objects on the cards begin with the same sound, the children should call out 'Snap!' The first child to say 'Snap!' can keep the pair, and the winner is the one with the most cards at the end of the game.

5. Bingo: 1

Age range
Five to six.
Group size
Pairs.
What you need
Two identical copies of a magazine, a sheet of card, adhesive, scissors.
What to do
Part of the benefit of this game comes from the preparation, which involves looking for things which are the same as each other.

Cut out 12 pieces of card which are small enough to take only one picture. Cut out a further two pieces of card which are large enough to take six pictures.

The children can then go through the two magazines and cut out the same 12 pictures from each. One set of pictures is mounted individually, and the other set is divided in half, so that six pictures are mounted on one of the large cards and six on the other. Children may need help with this part of the task.

In pairs, the children can now play the game. They should have one large card each; the individual cards are placed face down between the two children. They then take it in turns to turn over a small card. If it matches one on their large card they put it on top, and if not they return it to the middle, face down.

The winner is the one whose card is covered first.

6. Bingo: 2

Age range
Six to eight.
Group size
Pairs or groups of four or five.
What you need
Five cards 200mm × 100mm, 32 cards 50mm × 25mm.
What to do
Make two copies of 16 words you would like the children to recognise easily. Use words from your reading programme, from the 100 Keywords (see page 62), the 100 Essential Words for Spelling, or from a current topic.

Rule the large cards into 50mm × 25mm sections. Fill in the 16 words on one master card. On the remaining four, block out up to eight sections

on each card. Vary the spaces that are blocked out on different cards. If you want to use the cards for game two below, use the master card to fill the spaces with words. If you have covered fewer than eight spaces, make a third set of individual cards.

Game one
Four players each have a large card, and the individual cards are placed face down in the middle of the table. Each player takes it in turn to pick up a card. If the child can say the word, she places it on her card; if she cannot she returns it face down.

The winner is the first to fill her card.

Game two
In this game there are four players and a caller, who keeps the master card and the pack. As he turns over a card, the caller says the word and shows it to the players. The one who has the word written on his card says its name and places the word on his card. Any word that is not claimed, the caller places on his master card.

7. Make your own books: 1

Age range
Five to seven.
Group size
Small groups of up to four children.

What you need
A4 paper and felt-tipped pens.
What to do
Books which children can quickly make themselves become early reading books. They have more meaning for the children than conventional books because they are written in their own words and are about themselves and their lives. Also, as the children are helped to put the words on the page, they begin to understand how words come together to make meaning.

The easiest books to make are zigzag books. All you have to do is cut an A4 sheet of paper in half lengthways, fold each section in half and then in half again, to make two zigzag books. If you need a longer book, stick two sections together. The children can make their own zigzag books called 'All about me'. It may be best to start by working with pairs of children, but in time you will find that four is an

acceptable group. Each child can still have the help he needs and yet work individually on a letter or word he knows. It is very important to let the children do as much work as they can for themselves.

Write on the front of each zigzag book 'All about me, by...' and ask each child to write his own name. On the next page, after he has drawn a picture of himself, ask him how he wants to introduce himself, for example, 'I am Asim'. He may be able to write 'I', but if not then you can write it for him. If he knows that 'am' begins with 'a', let him write it with his finger on the table or

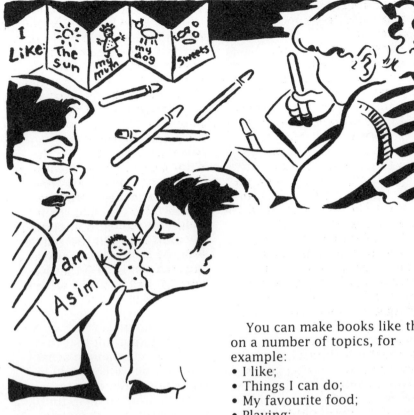

trace over a letter card before he writes it in his book. If he can write 'm', fine; if not, finish the word for him.

On the next page, he can draw something else about himself, and again you should help him with the text. Follow this pattern through the book, completing two pages at a session.

At the start of each session, read together the completed pages. If he wants a word he has used previously, encourage him to find it. Ask him to look at the tall letters, those with tails, those that sit on the line. After he has written it with his finger on the table, cover the word with your hand and ask him to write it from memory. If he gets stuck, give him a quick peep, but cover it up again.

You can make books like this on a number of topics, for example:
• I like;
• Things I can do;
• My favourite food;
• Playing;
• Watching;
• Stories I like.

Each child will add words to his reading and writing vocabulary with every book he makes; he will also build his confidence to use the words he knows. The collection of zigzag books can also go home to be read with parents, but make sure they are always returned to school for reading during the day.

Further activity
Once the children start to write more than three or four words, show them how to make writing books by cutting two sheets of A4 in half widthways to make A5, and then folding these smaller pieces in half. Cut a piece of card to the same size, fold, and staple it to the fold of the pages as a cover. Make sure the staple ends are tightly closed in the middle.

8. Make your own books: 2

Age range
Seven to eleven.
Group size
Individuals or pairs.
What you need
Book-making materials such as paper, cardboard, felt-tipped pens, pencils, stapler, needle and thread.
What to do
Throughout the primary years, develop the children's book-making skills so they proceed from zigzag books to booklets, and then to making proper stitched books to contain their stories, poems and topics.

When a child has made a book to hold her story, ask her to illustrate it, design the cover and write on the book the other details she would find in a shop-bought one. For example, she could write a synopsis of the book, say who produced it and how, and compose a pen portrait of the author. These story books should then be put among the published books on the book-shelves for others to read.

If a child has made a book for an anthology, encourage her to embellish each entry in a suitable way. The anthology could include her own poems along with published ones she has enjoyed reading.

9. Act it out

Age range
Five to seven.
Group size
The whole class or small groups.
What you need
A story your class knows and enjoys.
What to do
Choose a story that the children have heard many times before. Ask individual children to be the principal characters in the story, and then read the story to the children. Stop when you come to a piece of dialogue and allow the children to tell that section as they remember it. You can read the narrative.

On other occasions, ask individuals to act out the character parts and speak the dialogue while you provide the narrative link.

10. Kim's game

Age range
Five to seven.
Group size
Small groups.
What you need
Selection of small objects on a tray.
What to do
The development of a good visual memory is essential to both reading and writing. Use the following activity to help develop visual memory. Place ten objects on a tray and show them to the group. Check that everybody knows the names of all the objects, and tell them that you want them to remember them all. Ask the children to close their eyes and then remove one of the objects. See if the children can tell you which one is missing.
Further activity
• Remove two and then three objects at a time.
• Add first one, then add up to three objects.
• Increase the number of objects on the tray.
• Shorten the time you allow for transferring to memory.

11. Word wall

Age range
Five to eight.
Group size
The whole class.
What you need
Brick-shaped pieces of paper, an outline of a wall for each child, felt-tipped pens, adhesive.
What to do
Choose an appropriate initial letter or string and write it on the blackboard. Then ask the children to think of as many words as they can that begin with the same sound. The children can then copy each word on to a 'brick', and stick each brick in a space in their wall.

They can do several walls, but it is important that they do not complete them in school. Instead, the walls should be taken home and read to parents, who can help find further words to complete them. Completed walls must then be returned to school to share with the rest of the class.

12. Book tables

Age range
Five to eleven.
Group size
The whole class or individuals.
What you need
An attractively covered table, a box of strips of paper measuring about 5 × 20cm.
What to do
A book table draws attention to particular books, or to specific features of them, and so makes children more aware of the range and content of the books.

To make a book table, cover a small table with pastel or neutral-coloured textured paper or cloth and use some of the following suggestions.

• When you have read a story to the class, put the book on the table for them to read. Ask them to do the same with books they enjoy.

• Books that reinforce current work should also be put on the book table. For example, if you are working on descriptions of people or places, on senses or on dialogue or plot, direct the children to look out for good examples. If they find any, they should mark the place in the book with a strip of paper and head it with an appropriate title, such as 'people', 'place' or 'touch'. They can also add the title of the book and the page number if possible.

• If children have particularly enjoyed a book, ask them to put it on the table with a note saying why they enjoyed it.

• Choose an 'author of the week' and collect books and publishers' display material about the author and her books. Make the table look attractive with pictures and models made by the children based on the author's work.

13. Reading together

Age range
Six to eleven.
Group size
Four children.
What you need
Four copies of one book.
What to do
Give each of the four children in the group a copy of the same book. The children then read the book aloud together – never one child alone.

The group can be of mixed ability because the fluent readers ease forward the less able ones and help them to see what it is like to read fluently. Obviously the gap should not

be too wide, but some children will enjoy just being part of the group and following the story.

14. Using the library

Age range
Seven to eleven.
Group size
The whole class or small groups.
What you need
A good school library, organised for children's use, slips of paper, small bag or box.
What to do
Class task
At the beginning of every year, take the children into the library and explain how the books are set out, how they can find the books they need, how to take out and return books and what to do with damaged books. Explain where audio-visual equipment and topic boxes are stored and what the system is for borrowing and returning them.

Summarise the procedures and put them on the classroom information board.
Group task
Devise a 'lucky dip' where the children take from a bag or

box a slip of paper with an instruction written on it. They should then read the slip, return it to the bag and try to carry out the task. They may have to find a book or piece of equipment, and then show it to you and return it to its place.

Instructions could be:
• Find me a book by Nina Bawden.
• Find me three books about freshwater fish.
• Find me some information on emperor penguins.
• Return this encyclopaedia to its correct position on the shelf.
• Find a map of Europe.
• Return this film strip to its correct place.

These practice tasks need not take long, but they do familiarise children with the processes set up to keep the library tidy and organised. Watch how the children use the system, check how they observe procedures, and ask what else they need to know if you see that they have difficulties. Also, if children have problems, talk through with the staff how the library's organisation could be altered to make it easier.

If some of the children have used the library unsupervised, then it is often a good idea to go and check that they have left it tidy and orderly.

15. Helping children to choose fiction

Age range
Seven to eleven.
Group size
Individuals.
What you need
Access to a wide variety and range of reading materials, photocopiable page 154.
What to do
Browsing
When children are selecting books, talk to them individually about browsing. Tell them how to find out what

kinds of books are available and where they might be found. Discuss the value of picking up a book that looks interesting and dipping into it, or just looking at the pictures, to see whether they might like to read it.

Take the children to visit the local library so that they can browse there and learn to find their way around. This will help them to become more confident and to use the library in their own time, especially as some children may not have been given the chance to visit it before.
Choosing
Use the time when the children are choosing their books as an opportunity to talk with them about books.
• What books have they read?
• What did they like about them?
• What books do they usually read?
• What are they looking for this time?
Recording
Give each child a reading record sheet (photocopiable page 154) in which to enter the date, the name of the book, the author and a brief comment on each book they have read.

16. Five finger test

Age range
Seven to eleven.
Group size
Individuals.
What you need
No special requirement.
What to do
Children need help to assess a book and to tell whether it looks too difficult for them. If left to themselves they may judge on the wrong criteria. Big print or few words does not necessarily mean easier reading.

The following procedure is a simple but effective method by which children can easily learn to assess a book.
• Begin reading the first page.
• Hold up a finger for every word that is too difficult to read.
• If there are more than five on that page, the book is too difficult and another should be chosen.

If after having carried out this process they find that the book is too difficult but they would still like to read it, they can:
• take it home and read it with a parent or sibling;
• have it read to them at home;
• read it in school with an older or more fluent reader;
• have you read it to the class during story time.

17. Play detective

Age range
Seven to eleven.
Group size
Individuals, pairs or small groups.
What you need
A prepared story.
What to do
Decide on an area which you feel the children need to look at in their own fiction writing;

for example, cause and effect. Then choose some short stories (or parts of them) and devise questions that help children look deeper into them. This should help build up their understanding and use of cause and effect.

Use questions like the following:
• What happened when...?
• What made X change her mind?
• Why did ... happen?
• What kind of person was...?
• Why do you think he...?
• What do we know about...?

Write the questions on cards and put them into the books.

Tell the children you want them to read the story to enjoy it, and then to look at the questions. They can read the story again to find out the information they need to answer the questions.

18. Skimming and scanning

Age range
Seven to eleven.
Group size
Whole class or small groups.
What you need
Access to a school or class library.
What do do
Skimming and scanning are important skills for children to learn, since they are the means by which we find information to answer our questions. Introduce the children to the following procedures for locating information.

Skimming
Skimming is one way of establishing what a text is about, in order to decide whether we need to read it, and if so, which parts are important. Our eye runs quickly down the page seeking words which relate to our need.

Before children start to skim a text for information, they must know what questions they are asking of the text, and the purposes to which the information will be put. Having decided that, they can use the library's organisational system to locate a book that could be useful.

A book's contents list, chapter titles and sub-headings can all be used to see whether the book covers the specific information sought. If there is an index, the children can use that to locate the information more accurately.

When skimming text, children will find that illustrations, photographs and diagrams may help in locating possible areas of information.
Scanning
Scanning is the way we look at a particular passage of text to locate the part we need to read with close attention.

When they have located a section that may contain the information they need, introduce the children to the technique of reading the first sentence of a paragraph to see whether they need to read further.

If the paragraph seems relevant, encourage the children to scan the passage by sweeping their eyes lightly but systematically over it, rather like a radar beam. This way they can decide whether the passage merits close attention or whether they have to seek further.

CHAPTER 3

Writing

Writing is a medium through which we can communicate our thoughts. Writing our ideas down helps to develop our thinking, and also stimulates our responses as we pause to reflect. Thus it becomes easier to deal with complex ideas and examine connections, and to be more exact in our thinking. It is possible to think on paper, throw ideas around, make and remake, and so define and refine our thinking.

Writing is a skill we use all our lives in one form or another. It is a medium through which we tell others what we know, and a means by which they can then assess our knowledge and competence.

When we speak we don't have to think about what the words look like, but when we write we not only have to think about what we want to say, but also about spelling, handwriting, the spaces between words and the various written ways of conveying features of spoken language such as stress and intonation.

In recent years the teaching of writing has changed radically, moving from formal practices and exercises, through 'creative writing', to concern for the process of writing itself. Children are encouraged to behave like 'real' writers, to get down their ideas, to redraft, edit and then present their work in a form best suited to its purpose and audience.

BACKGROUND

Written communication begins with scribble. Gradually pictures form, then letters and words begin to emerge. As children's knowledge of written language grows, so the words they write come closer to what they want to say.

Once they begin to express themselves in words, children need a wide variety of opportunities through which they can grow into confident and practised writers. They need opportunities to become proficient at expressing their thinking in clear, accurate writing suited to both audience and purpose.

Children cannot learn everything at once; the harder the task the more errors they are likely to make. The easier the task the more control they have over the choice of words, grammar, spelling and punctuation.

Writing can be made easier if its subject matter can be seen, touched or experienced; it also helps if it has a beginning, a middle and an end. A story, a personal experience, a science experiment or the instructions for a game have an internal pattern, a recognisable sequence, a chronological order, through which the writing proceeds.

Non-chronological writing lacks these 'hooks'; consequently, it takes longer to develop to an equivalent standard.

Composing is at the heart of all writing. Having composed the content, the writer can organise and improve it, but it is how we compose a piece of writing that makes it good or bad.

To be effective across the writing spectrum, then, children must learn how to:
• write coherently over a wide range of topics, issues, incidents and ideas;
• write in different genres, such as stories, poetry, messages, accounts, plays, instructions, essays and reports, and organise and present work in different ways so that it engages the reader;
• describe events, factual or fictional, and present them coherently and chronologically;
• plan and present information in a variety of ways, for example through modelling or matrices;
• recognise the different kinds of uses to which writing is put in adult life.

All these aspects of writing can be introduced to children at an early age, and can then be built on throughout the primary years.

In this chapter we shall look at ideas for developing writing genres for a wide range of purposes, and also at techniques for redrafting and conferencing.

ACTIVITIES

1. Cards for all reasons

Age range
All ages.

Group size
Individuals, pairs, small groups or the whole class.

What you need
Good quality cartridge paper or thin card, felt-tipped pens, scraps of material, paper.

What to do
Most children will make a card with very little encouragement. Cards can be made for Christmas, birthdays, Mothers' or Fathers' Day, St Valentine's Day, Easter, when someone is leaving, or when congratulations are due.

A seasonal or topical message can be written inside and a suitable picture or a colourful collage put on the front. Cut the paper to the required size for the younger ones.

Older children can write a suitable verse for the card bearing in mind the intended recipient.

2. Directions

Age range
All ages.

Group size
Pairs or small groups.

What you need
No special requirements.

What to do
Discuss with the children how they get from their classroom to the playground, or the toilets, or the Head's study. Which way do they go?

Young children can 'make the pencil show the way to go' by drawing the way with paper and pencil, making a line twist and turn as the route turns. Older children can write down the directions, and then pass them to a friend to draw a map according to the instructions.

Further activity
Move on to other topics such as:
• The way I come to school.
• The way to the shops/library/supermarket/post office/park/my friend's house.

Again, the younger children can draw the route and older ones write the directions for others to draw the map of the route.

3. Picture collection

Age range
Six to eleven.

Group size
Individuals, pairs and small groups.

What you need
Collections of interesting pictures, photographs and postcards, card, transparent self-adhesive plastic film.

What to do
Mount each picture on card and cover with transparent film. Gradually, with the children's help, your set of pictures will build into a fascinating collection. Many pictures can be obtained free, but superb photographs can also be bought from specialist companies.

On the back of each picture card write an alphabetical list of words that might be helpful to the children. Don't write words that you would expect them to be able to write unaided, or words they can build up or look up with ease. Ask them to look up the words you have written before they use them, so that they can check that the word is the one they want.

The children can then use the cards to help them invent characters, places and food in stories, poems and descriptive writing, and as a stimulus for posters, advertisements and so on – the list is endless.

4. Picture lists

Age range
Five to six.
Group size
Pairs or small groups.
What you need
Magazines, mail order catalogues, scissors, adhesive, paper, pencils.
What to do
The children should decide what kind of list they want to make; for example, 'clothes to wear', 'food for dinner', 'things for our baby' etc. They can then cut out pictures according to the category they have chosen and stick them, one underneath the other, on a sheet of paper.

Beside each picture the children should attempt to write what it shows.

5. Lists

Age range
Six to nine.
Group size
Pairs or small groups.
What you need
Pencils and papers.
What to do
We are all list makers of one sort or another. Lists serve a number of useful purposes in planning, remembering and helping to get things done. List making is a useful tool for children to acquire which will help them throughout their lives.

In connection with a topic or class work, devise a number of real purposes for making lists or *aides-mémoires*. For example, the children could make a list of things to have for a packed lunch, words to learn to spell, kit for PE, ingredients for cooking, tasks to be done, areas to cover in a topic, tasks to be completed, friends they would like to come to a party, presents they had for Christmas, and so on. Other 'wishful thinking' lists could include 'Things I would like to do', 'Five people I would most like to meet', 'Ten places I would like to visit', 'Five things I might be when I'm grown up' and so on. Children could also state why they wanted to do these things.

Lists written for imaginary purposes would include, 'In my Christmas stocking I found...', 'At the supermarket I bought...', 'The ten things I would find most useful on a desert island are...'.

6. Thirteen ways

Age range
Five to seven.
Group size
Whole class or small groups.
What you need
White board, flip chart or blackboard, paper, pencils.
What to do
Read to the children some of the verses from 'Thirteen Ways of Looking at a Teddy Bear' in *Word Games* by Sandy Brownjohn and Janet Whitaker (Hodder and Stoughton). Emphasise that there are many different ways of looking at the world around us.

Choose a subject between you – a toy, a creature, Mum, Dad, a brother or sister, school – and talk together about your feelings towards the subject, what the subject looks like, what you could do with it and so on.

Having talked in such detail children are ready to make statements about what the subject means or represents to them. Talk about each statement and work it through with them. Write each one on the board so words or line lengths can be changed and read them through together. Four or five statements will be enough to start with. Copy out the statements on a piece of paper and pin it up low enough for the children to point to the words as they read them through.

The children can draw pictures for each statement to go into a booklet with a 'verse' and a picture on facing pages. This booklet could be taken home and read with parents.

Further activity

Ask the children each to choose their own subject and think of one thing that is special about it. They should then write down any phrases which come to mind and use them to create a verse. When they have finished one verse they can think about the subject in a different way – its size, shape, colour, the way it moves, how it makes them feel, what it makes them think of – and write verses around these thoughts. Children can also work together by taking turns to write a line for each theme.

The children could write their own 'Thirteen ways ...' poems, for example, 'Thirteen ways of cleaning your feet', and so on.

7. This is my life

Age range
Seven to eleven.
Group size
Individuals.
What you need
Large sheets of paper, pencils.
What to do
Read 'The End' ('When I was One') from A. A. Milne's *Now We are Six*. Discuss whether it tells you anything about Christopher Robin.

Ask the children to make time lines from sheets of paper cut into wide strips. They should divide the strips into equal sections, each of which represents a year of the child's life.

The children should take home their time lines and discuss with their parents the happenings in their life. They then select what they feel to be important from each year, and write it in the year spaces of their time line. The events may be big, like moving house, or small, like cutting a tooth, or serious, like having an accident.

Further activity
The time lines can be put up together, and examined for similarity of events. Ask the children to tabulate or write up the similarities and differences.

8. Personal diaries, journals and logs

Age range
Seven to eleven.
Group size
Individuals.
What you need
Blank books, photocopiable pages 155 and 156.
What to do
Introduce the topic by reading to the children some poems about the days of the week. For example, with younger children read 'Monday's child' or 'Solomon Grundy', and with older children 'The gas man cometh' (Flanders and Swan).

Keep a diary of school events, as well as a timetable, up on the wall at child-height, and discuss with the children what they do on different days. Ask them to keep a diary for one week, using photocopiable page 155, and then to compare it with others in their group.

Ask the children to keep a journal or log book, writing about things that happen, world events or personal dilemmas. They could use page 156 to record details of their favourite television programmes. Alternatively they could try to keep a

commonplace book, including words, phrases and passages collected from books, a well-drawn image, a noteworthy or telling experience; anything that has impressed them and could make good copy. They should add scraps of overheard dialogue, anecdotes, puns and other plays on language. Remind the children to date their entries and to keep their books, as they may come in useful later.

9. Letters

Age range
All ages.

Group size
Individuals.

What you need
A5 size notepaper or half sheets of coloured A4 photocopy paper, pens or pencils.

What to do
Letters, at the earliest stage, have three parts:
• hello (who it is to);
• the message (what it is for);
• goodbye (who it is from).
Older children's letters should have four parts:
• the address;
• the greeting;
• the message;
• the farewell.

The children should decide what they want to write and put it down in rough. After checking with you, and redrafting as necessary, they can write the letter carefully on notepaper. Older children can learn to address the envelopes. Put samples up in the writing corner for the children to refer to.

Find as many reasons for writing letters as possible. The children could write:
• to parents about a school event, visit or day closure;
• to thank a visitor;
• to thank another class for their assembly or show or the books they made;
• to say thank you to someone who has helped them;
• to apologise to someone they have hurt or been rude to;
• for business purposes connected with enterprise schemes;

- to enquire about visits;
- to ask for information;
- to complain about faulty goods or breakdowns;
- to pen-pals across the world.

Writing letters from fictional characters or famous people can be fun. Try the following ideas:
- Write a letter from King Midas saying thank you for the golden touch.
- Write a letter from Wilbur, thanking Charlotte for being his friend (see *Charlotte's Web*, by E. B. White, Puffin).
- Write a letter from Tyke Tyler, thanking the Headmaster for the potted plant or apologising for the damage she caused (see *The Turbulent Term of Tyke Tyler*, by Gene Kemp, Puffin).

As you can see, there is plenty of scope for writing letters. It is important that you convey the fact that letters contain many different kinds of messages.

10. Wish you were here

Age range
Six to eleven.
Group size
Individuals.
What you need
Card about 150 × 100cm, divided in two on one side, felt-tipped pens, world map, postcards sent to school.
What to do
Put up a display of postcards, some showing the pictures and some the messages. Tell the children to pretend that they are on holiday or at camp and must send a card home saying what an exciting time they are having.

Show them how to address a card and talk about the kinds of messages that could be written. Encourage older pupils to inject humour and local detail into their message. If they have chosen a faraway place they should research the location to find places of interest nearby which they could write about and illustrate on their card.

They could also write a card to an imaginary person extolling the pleasures of their home town, adding an illustration of a local monument or beauty spot.

11. One way into poetry

Age range
Five to seven when used as a class activity; seven to eleven when used with individuals or pairs.
Group size
Individuals, pairs or whole class.
What you need
Magnifying glasses, small natural or man-made object.
What to do
Leave an object and a magnifying glass on display

and ask children to have a good look at the object during the day. They can touch, smell and shake it – if the object will survive the onslaught!

Later that day, gather the children together. On the board write the figures one to five, one below the other. Ask the children questions like the following, and discuss the answers until they are satisfied with them.
• What colour is it?
• What does it look like?
• What does it make you think of?
• What would you use it for?
• How light or heavy is it?

Write the answers on the board and see whether they can be worked into a poem. You can copy out the poem and put it up at the children's eye-height for them to read for themselves.

12. Colours

Age range
Five to eight.
Group size
Whole class and small groups.
What you need
A display of objects all the same colour, some pieces of card for labels, pens.
What to do
Choose a colour, say red, and ask the children to find as many things in the room as

they can that are red. When they have found them they should put them on the display table and write a label for the item; for example, 'A red block'. Write 'Red is' on the board and ask 'What is red?' Each sentence they give you must start with 'Red is ...'.

The children can then write a short statement beginning 'Red is ...' and you can put their sentences together in pairs or fours so that they make a poem. You could link the verses together by giving them the same last line, for example, 'I like red things'. The poem can then be mounted on a suitable backing such as a huge red tomato.
    'Red is a tomato, juicy and round,
    Red is a leaf down on the ground,
    I like red things.'

A red tomato   A red block   A red handkerchief   A red shoe

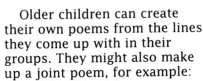

Older children can create their own poems from the lines they come up with in their groups. They might also make up a joint poem, for example:

'Red is a letter-box,
Its mouth open wide,
Hundreds of letters
Tumble inside.'

This idea can be repeated in numerous ways for other colours, shapes, sizes, places, Mums, Dads, seasonal things like snow and frost... the list is endless.

13. My treasure

Age range
Nine to eleven.
Group size
Individuals.
What you need
Poetry rough book and pencil, personal treasure (optional).
What to do
Spend a few minutes discussing with the whole class what a treasure is, what things you and the children treasure and why. If you have brought a treasure, share it with them, and if you have written a poem about it share that too.

Ask the children to think of something they treasure, and to close their eyes for two minutes and visualise it. Ask them to 'brainstorm' phrases that come into their heads as they think about their treasure (see Activity 29, page 53). They can then write down how they came by their treasure and why it is special to them.

Ask the children to write a poem about their treasure,

using both the phrases and the prose. Once they have it down in rough, ask them to go through it and remove as many 'little' words such as 'a', 'an' and 'the' as they can, and rewrite it. They can then share what they have written with a neighbour, reading it out and asking them if the meaning is clear and whether any changes could be made.

Every draft should be in their poetry rough book so they can see how the poem developed and keep track of good phrases which might get lost in the redrafting.

14. Haiku

Age range
Nine to eleven.
Group size
Individuals or pairs.
What you need
A selection of haiku poems.
What to do
A haiku is a Japanese form of poetry, usually illustrated, which is made up of three lines and seventeen syllables. The first line of the poem has five syllables, the second line seven, and the third line five syllables.

These poems were originally word pictures of an aspect of nature, though today they cover a wider range of subject matter.

Read haiku poems to your class, discussing each line and what it expresses, but keeping sight of the overall picture. Next, explore the syllabic content of the lines by clapping or tapping along to the rhythm. Then ask the children to think of words that would fit a first line; for example, 'Two green aliens', or 'Imagination'.

Choose one of the suggestions and write it at the top of the board. Then ask for suggestions for line two, writing them across the middle of the board. Whittle them down to three or four, cutting out 'loose' words, and then work on a last line.

The poems could take the following form:
• Line 1 – sets the scene;
• Line 2 – focuses on something in it;
• Line 3 – compares it with something.
An alternative form might be:
• Line 1 – a comment on nature;

Double, double, toil and trouble...

Spells

• Line 2 – a linked statement;
• Line 3 – what they add up to. Haiku poems are ideal for handwriting practice, and should have an illustration which adds to the theme.

15. Spells and incantations

Age range
Seven to nine.
Group size
Pairs or groups of four.
What you need
Pencils and paper.
What to do
Witches in stories, witches' chants and spells, Hallowe'en and music like 'The Sorcerer's Apprentice' all help to set the scene for making up spells and incantations.

The rhythm of spells and incantations is very simple and regular, with either two or four beats to each line, and rhyme at the end of each fourth beat. Because of the simplicity of the form, children are unlikely to force the rhyme.

The incantation from Shakespeare's *Macbeth* is well worth exploring; young children love getting their tongue round the venomous phrases.

The children can make up their own phrases and write them on strips of paper. These strips can then be put together to form a spell.
Further activity
Make up a two-line stanza to lead into the spell, and one or two lines at the end to show the power of the spell.

16. Writing about the senses

Age range
Seven to eleven.
Group size
Individuals or small groups.
What you need
No special requirements.
What to do
We can develop our appreciation of our senses by thinking, talking and writing about them, and through close observation of the world around us. Children's language skills will be enriched if they are encouraged to use their senses to the full.

The work in this section leads on from the activity on talking about the senses in Chapter 1 (pages 14 and 15). Before starting the activity, show or remind the children how to brainstorm for words to help them in their writing.
Sight
Start by asking the children to find all the alternatives they can for the word 'see'.

After exploring things they can see from a fairly broad viewpoint such as the street, the playground, the classroom, the entrance hall or the library, narrow the focus to one thing. How many things can they notice about a large tree, the adventure playground, the front of a building, the greengrocer's shop...?

Narrow the focus again and ask the children to observe even more closely:
• a leaf;
• a branch of a tree;
• an animal at the zoo;
• a flower;
• a watch or clock.

Provide magnifying glasses so that the children can examine every little visual detail and record it in the most descriptive terms. Suggest they look at the object's size, shape, colour, texture, the way it moves and so on, recording what they see as accurately as possible.
Sound
Ask the children to make a collection of words descriptive of sound, such as 'noise', 'din', 'tune', 'cry', 'crash', 'click', 'tinkle', 'melodic', 'vocal', etc.

Start them writing about

sounds in broad themes such as the following:
- digging up the road;
- getting dinner;
- playtime;
- going home;
- firework night.

Move to more specific sounds:
- frying bacon;
- opening a parcel;
- cleaning one's teeth;
- a mechanical toy;
- a clock ticking;
- a mosquito in the bedroom.

Ask the children to create, in their own words, a sound picture to capture these moments.

Touch

Set up a table with objects of different textures brought by you and the children. Provide a strip of paper beside each item on which children can write words to describe the texture of that item.

Then ask the children to make a collection of alternative words for touch using dictionaries, thesauruses and glossaries.

Touch lends itself easily to imagery; for example, 'as soft as silk', 'as smooth as glass'. Encourage children to think of less usual but equally apt imagery for everyday items or for things on the touch table. Themes for writing on the subject of touch could include 'Things I love or hate to touch and why', 'Investigating a Christmas stocking in the dark', and so on.

Alternatively, ask the children to imagine they are entering a room that is very familiar to them but in total darkness. They should write down the feel of the items they touch as they try to move around the room.

Taste

Ask the children to make a collection of words to describe taste, using glossaries, dictionaries and thesauruses to find alternatives.

Bring in items of food like jelly, carrots, apples, chews and toffee for the children to eat. They should describe what happens to each sort of food in their mouth.

Ask the children to:
- write 'taste' labels for exotic party food;
- describe the food they would eat at a Roman or Mediaeval banquet;
- design an advertisement for a new kind of sweet or ice-cream;
- pretend they are a space alien and write about eating a banana for the very first time;
- write a letter to a pen-friend far away describing their favourite food.

Smell

Ask the children to make a list of words to use as alternatives to smell, words like 'fragrance', 'aroma', 'stink', 'pungence', 'bouquet', 'breath', 'whiff', 'sniff', 'scent', 'reek' and 'odour'.

Stimulus materials can be brought in, such as lemon juice, seaweed, flowers, fruit, polish, mild disinfectant, coffee, mint, pickles, moth-balls, leather, spices and herbs to stimulate the olfactory organs. Ask the children to describe these distinctive smells as graphically as possible.

Smelly themes for children to explore individually or in groups could include:
- the seaside;
- my favourite shop;
- my Mum's cooking;
- in a fish and chip shop;
- at the farm.

Ask them to design an advertisement for something aromatic or pungent.

17. In the news

Age range
Nine to eleven.
Group size
Individuals.
What you need
Several different daily papers.
What to do
Discuss a current topic or event, perhaps on an ecological theme. Ask the children to watch the news for information about the topic, and to try to read about it in the daily press. They can also discuss it with their parents.

Ask the children to bring in copies of any relevant articles they have found to share with classmates. Some background information might be found in the library, or sought from embassies if appropriate.

The children should read the articles paragraph by paragraph, making notes of the most important items or phrases in each one. To these notes they can add any information gained from other sources.

They should then try to write their own article on the topic.
Further activity
This method of writing topical articles can be used for writing about fashion, music, books, films, trade, law or travel.

18. Planning non-fiction

Age range
Nine to eleven.
Group size
Individuals, pairs or small groups.
What you need
Paper and pencils.
What to do
Ask the children to list all they know or have found out about a chosen topic. They should list the items irrespective of order, placing each point on a separate line. They can then decide which of these points has to be written about first, and write the figure one beside it. Then they should number the rest in the most sensible order.

The children should write as much as they can about point number one before going on to number two. Each point can be crossed through when it has been written up. This text

should then be redrafted, and a neat copy made.

You will need to work through this technique a few times with the class before the children are ready to use it in small groups. It is a useful planning tool and prepares them for much of the writing they will undertake later on.

19. Plays

Age range
Six to eight.
Group size
Individuals, pairs and small groups.
What you need
Paper and pencils.
What to do
Using well-known conversations from fairy tales, folk tales, Aesop's fables etc, the children can discuss what is said. They should elect one child in the group to write down who said what in play form, like this:
'Little Red Riding Hood (LRRH) and the wolf meet at Grandma's house.
LRRH: Oh, Grandma, what big eyes you've got.
WOLF: All the better to see you with, my dear.
LRRH: Oh, Grandma, what ...'.
Working this way children begin to explore the technique of play writing without the difficulty of composing at the same time.

20. Play writing

Age range
Eight to eleven.
Group size
Pairs.
What you need
No special requirements.
What to do
Ask the children to act out a pretend conversation. The topic for the conversation can

be generated by the children, or you could choose a suitable one. They could pretend to be having a telephone conversation, or they could be an old person and a young one in conversation, or two people taking part in a sport, a show, a film, a hard sell, etc.

The children should act out the scene in character. They can work on the script and refine it until they are satisfied, and then write it in play form. The script can be enacted in front of the class and then made into a booklet for others to use.

21. Picture stories

Age range
Five to seven.
Group size
Individuals or pairs.
What you need
Paper, pencils, crayons or felt-tipped pens.
What to do
Picture stories are one way in which the beginnings of both story and play writing can be developed.

Ask the children to draw pictures of themselves doing something, or something happening to them. Discuss with them what is happening in the picture, and what the person in the picture is saying. Encourage the children to write the speech on the picture beside the face, and to draw a speech bubble around the words. They can then write underneath the picture what is happening.

The children can try the activity again, but this time they should fold the paper in half widthways. On the first half of the paper they should draw a picture of themselves doing something. Discuss what might happen next, and ask them to draw this on the other half of the paper. Again they should add speech bubbles and write a sentence under each picture to say what is happening.

The children can then move on to folding their paper in three. This time their first picture should try to set the scene, the second should show something happening and the third should show how it ended.

A longer strip can then be made if you wish, with more picture spaces to allow for the beginning, the first event, its effect, what that caused to happen and the result.

Children often spend a long time on the beginning of a story, not enough on the middle and virtually no time on the end. This picture method of developing story writing helps children to think through a story and give proper weight to each part.

Further activity
When the concept of picture stories has been grasped, you can use this form of composition as a stimulus for play writing. Ask the children to draw a picture of an event, with at least two people in it. They should write in speech bubbles on the picture the first thing each character says, and write the names of the characters below the picture. Then the children can write what each character says next beside the name.

If the children are working in pairs, they can talk through the characters' dialogue together.

This technique can be used as a planning device around which plays can be built.

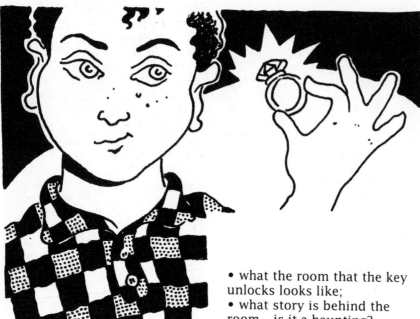

22. Story starters

Age range
Eight to eleven.
Group size
Whole class.
What you need
An item to stimulate the children's interest, such as an interesting-looking key or an unusual ring.
What to do
You can use a wide range of objects as starting points for stories, to stimulate the children's imagination. The following suggestions are examples of the sort of thing that is possible.

Mount the key on a piece of card and fix it to the blackboard. Tell the children to pretend that they have just found the key at the bottom of a trunk. Ask them to investigate:
• which house the key comes from;
• who lives there;
• what the house is like;

• what the room that the key unlocks looks like;
• what story is behind the room – is it a haunting?

The children can develop their ideas into a mystery story or newspaper article.

If you use the ring, either wear it or have it on display. Tell the children that it has magical powers, which will enable them to become superhuman if they rub it three times and say the magic words.

First they must go and write an incantation to summon from the ring the powers they wish to acquire. After rubbing the ring, they should then write an adventure story based on using their newly acquired magic powers.

23. Mystery parcels

Age range
Six to eleven.
Group size
Individuals or pairs.
What you need
An object in a padded envelope for each child in the group, for example, thimble, wooden toy, photograph, postcard, tiny book, etc.

What to do
Find a series of small items and put them in the envelopes. Seal each package. Ask each child to choose a package and feel it. They should then write down what they think might be inside it, how it feels, and how they feel.

Once the children have done this ask them to open the package without saying a word and explore it. They can then brainstorm a list of words that spring to mind. Next ask them to write down what the object is, and their thoughts on finding this out.

Numerous opportunities for writing spring from this activity, which can take place over several days. The class can:
• write a letter of thanks for the gift;
• write a description of it;
• write about how it was manufactured or made;
• write who they would like to give it to and why;
• write a poem about it;
• write a story in which the gift features;
• write a letter of complaint about a fault in it;
• list the different uses to which it can be put, real, imaginative and nonsensical;
• write to a friend inviting her to the grand unveiling of the gift;
• write the story of the journey of the gift to them. (This can be very fanciful!)

The children can make books of the different pieces of writing or display them.

24. Lost and found

Age range
Seven to eleven.
Group size
Whole class or small groups.

What you need
'Lost and found' advertisements from newspapers.
What to do
Ask the children to bring in 'lost and found' columns from their local paper or copies of cards in the local shops.

Ask them if they have ever lost something very special, or found something that could have been of value to someone else. Tell them to concentrate on one thing they would hate to lose and design an advertisement to ask for its return.

Encourage the children to write fanciful advertisements too, for example: 'Lost: flesh-eating piranha only ten feet long, harmless except for occasional bite. Box No. l02-9384'.

Display the advertisements on a lost and found column in the classroom.

Further activity
Suggest that the children respond to the advertisements in an imaginative way. They could:
• write a letter saying that they have found the missing item;
• write a feature article on how the item came to be lost or found;
• write a feature on the owner's response when the missing item is returned;
• write a feature on an exhibition of similar items;
• as the owner, write a letter to thank the person who found the lost item.

25. Planning a story

Age range
Seven to eleven.
Group size
Individuals, pairs and small groups.

What you need
A4 paper, pencils, photocopiable page 157.
What to do
Introduce the children to the idea of planning a story. There are a number of ways to do this, including using questions, options and flow charts.
Questions
The usual questions to ask are 'What happened?', 'Where?', 'When?', 'How?' and 'Why?'. Using a sheet of A4 paper, the children should space these five questions down the left-hand side. Underneath each heading they can then write the answer to each question. This becomes the bare outline for a rough draft. Alternatively, the children could use photocopiable page 157 to plan their stories.

Another approach is to answer a series of 'what if ...' questions. What if Butch slips his leash out in the street? What if he dashes across the roads and causes cars to toot their horns? What if a thief steals a purse while people are attracted to the furore? What if the thief runs away and Butch gives chase thinking it a game? What if he leaps at the man and knocks him to the ground?

After making a rough draft, reworking the text and redrafting, the children can write and illustrate the story.
Options
On a large piece of paper, ask the children to write an event or happening in the top left-hand corner. Beside it they can list four courses of action that could be undertaken. Then ask them to select one, and list four things that could result from that course of action.

They select one option and list four possible results, and so on until the story ends.

What happened	Options
Jake went out for a ride on his bike.	1. Meets a friend. 2. Gets lost. 3. Falls off. 4. Has a puncture.
He met his friend Bill.	1. Shopping for his mum. 2. Running away. 3. Going to play football. 4. Going swimming
Bill was running away.	

This outline becomes the plot of the story from which a rough draft can be made. The children will be fascinated by the many different stories which can be created from the same initial event.

The same idea can be used with younger children, but you will need to work with them in small groups. Devise an options chart with them for a picture from one of your collections (see page 28) or an event suggested by one of the group. Take suggestions from the group and let them discuss whether the ideas are possible within the confines of the story line. When the chart is finished the children can write the story in pairs.

This method reinforces the concept of cause and effect, the basis of all story writing.

Flow charts
A flow chart is a way of asking questions in order to develop the story. Who is the main character? What is the character's goal? What action is taken? Is the goal achieved? How does the story end?

The process of 'action to take', 'no' is gone through as many times as necessary until a 'yes' is achieved (see the chart below).

Each stage must be written down so that the movements of the plot are not lost, and a working draft can then be prepared.

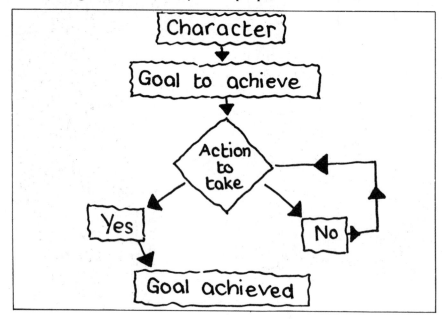

26. Places in stories: 1

Age range
Six to eight.
Group size
Individuals, pairs and small groups.
What you need
Pencils, paper.
What to do
Retell a familiar story and discuss in detail with the children the setting used for the story. Where was it set? Was the place important to the story, or could it have happened anywhere?

Think about places in other stories, like the Three Bears' house, the witch's house from 'Hansel and Gretel', the bridge from 'Three Billy Goats Gruff', or the rubbish tip from *Stig of the Dump* by Clive King (Puffin).

Then, with the children, imagine a place of your own which might be a good setting for a story. What sort of thing do the children think could happen there?

Ask them to write a description of this place, or of another place they have imagined, and decorate their writing with pictures if they like.

Finally, the children can write a story about the adventures which might have taken place in that imaginary setting.

27. Places in stories: 2

Age range
Nine to eleven.
Group size
Individuals, pairs and small groups.

What you need

Pictures of different places – postcards, pictures from travel magazines, specifications from estate agents with the address blocked out, and so on.

What to do

Using the collection of pictures, ask the children to imagine what it would be like to live in one of the places shown, and then to write a description of it.

Further activity

When children come across a particularly good piece of description in their reading ask them to share it or put a marker in it and, when they have finished the book, to put it on the book table for others to enjoy.

Ask the children to create an imaginary setting for different types of stories; adventure, travel, family, animal or sci-fi.

28. Characters in stories

Age range
Seven to eleven.

Group size
Individuals or small groups.

What you need

Clothing and props, for example, an overall, broom and duster, or jacket, trousers, pen, briefcase etc; coat hanger or tailor's dummy.

What to do

Warn the children that they are going to have a visitor. Say that you don't know much about the person except the day that the visitor is expected.

On the appointed day, have a set of clothing hanging from a hanger or a dummy ready for when the children arrive. Complete the outfit by adding any accessories, and on a table beside the dummy give clues to the likes, dislikes, occupation, hobbies and habits of the guest; for example, a letter, a theatre or show programme, a business magazine, a computer disc, a dentist's drill, a needle and cotton, a musical instrument, a stethoscope, a duster, a wooden spoon, a family or childhood photograph, a paint brush, a compass or a roll of film and so on.

After the children have had time to examine the artefacts, ask them to write a character study using all they know and all they can assume about the 'guest'. Then ask the children to write a story around the character.

29. Brainstorming

Age range
Eight to eleven.

Group size
Whole class.

What you need
Pencil, paper or work book, stopwatch.

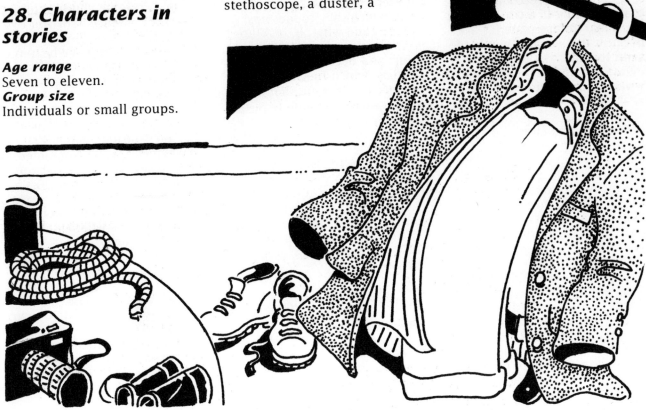

What to do
Brainstorming is a technique used to bring words and ideas into focus before starting to write.

It is better to record the brainstorming in a writing work book than to use paper, because this enables pupils to keep together the different ideas involved in developing writing, so that they can refer back to them when seeking stimuli.

The children should first fold their page lengthways once or twice, depending on the page width. Then you can ask them to think of some words that conjure up pictures in their minds. Decide on one word, and ask all the children to write this word at the top of their first column.

Then give the children two minutes to write as many words related to the first word as they can think of. Some children will fill half a column, others two or more, and the words do not have to be topic-related. Give the children a 30-second warning when their time is nearly up, and don't forget to write a list yourself. Then the children can compare lists, and when they have finished they can add any words that appeal to them from each other's lists.

Once the children have compiled several lists using different topics, discuss with them which they found most difficult and why.

You can also select a specific topic, and decide with the children which four words related to this topic should head up each column. Give the children five minutes to write as many words as they can that could loosely be connected with the leading word in each column.

Use this technique to help the children find words or phrases before they begin writing poetry, and the words will run much more readily off the pencil.

30. Redrafting

Age range
Five to eleven.
Group size
Individuals.
What you need
Paper and pencils.

What to do
Redrafting is a skill that can be taught to young children as well as to older ones. When children's scribble moves from left to right across the paper and letters appear in their writing, we can help them to start to look more closely at their writing.

When working with five- to six-year-olds, always ask the children to read their writing back to you, and when they do so, comment on the message. If they have written from left to right, or are beginning to use letters appropriately, praise them for what they have done correctly. They quickly learn what you are expecting from them.

After they have read their 'writing' to you, ask if you may respond to the text in your writing. Say the words very clearly as you write them down. Invite the children to read the sentence with you two or three times.

When children have begun to produce their own written work, redrafting can make it look very messy, but writing on alternate lines creates space for changes and means fewer mistakes during rewriting.

When they have completed a piece of work, children should read it through. By acting as a reader children become aware of words they have left out, and can assess whether the text hangs together and whether it expresses what they want to say. They notice parts that need to be altered, misspellings and punctuation errors. By redrafting their own writing children learn that writing is not sacrosanct; it can be developed and changed.

Devise a check card to help children look systematically through their work. Use questions which cover what the children already know.

When they have checked their work carefully, children are then ready to talk with you, their peers or a helper, and be helped to look at meaning, clarity and consistency of story line, punctuation and grammar. Ask them why they made changes and discuss the effect upon the text. This will help them to look critically at their writing and analyse the effect of changes.

Of course, not all writing needs to be redrafted, but if the idea of change and development is established at a young age, redrafting becomes a natural part of writing. Children not only become more critical of their own work and that of others, but also develop a growing awareness of what makes good writing.

31. Conferencing

Age range
All ages.
Group size
Individuals.
What you need
No special requirements.
What to do
When children are busy writing, move around the class talking quietly with individuals about how they are getting on, whether they are happy with the way their work is going and what they will write next. The technical aspects can be looked at later; at this point you just want them to get their ideas down.

Spend only a few minutes with each pupil. The whole idea is to keep them moving forward, not slowing to a halt and then rejecting the task.

To take the idea of conferences one stage further, date a piece of A4 paper and

pin it up for children to sign when they are ready for a conference. Tick off names as you work with the children, to help you to keep track of who you have seen and how often.

Choose a quiet corner and sit beside the child. Ask if you may read his work. Older pupils may not be ready to share it with you at that time, but they might be willing to talk about it. Return the work to the pupil so that he keeps ownership of it and of any changes that may be made. Ask an open-ended question like 'How's it going?', to start the conversation off. Children quickly get used to working this way and come prepared.

The important thing is to follow the child. It is the child's writing, so he must decide how it should develop. This does not mean that your role is passive; you have to listen carefully to understand what he wants to achieve. Do not be afraid to give your opinions, or to ask the kind of question that can lead the child out of a difficulty, but don't jump in too quickly. A couple of minutes may seem a long time to wait, but reflection takes time, and writing development is directly related to the child's ability to reflect.

Once the composing is finished, the technical aspects can be attended to. Real writing growth quickly becomes evident, along with a change of attitude towards writing. Additionally, as this way of working becomes established, children recognise its value and perceive the need not to interrupt when you are conferencing with another child.

CHAPTER 4

Spelling

It is important that children are able to write quickly and accurately, and can put down on paper what they want to say without unnecessary hindrance. To do this they need to be freed from the concept that every word they write must be spelled correctly the first time around. This does not mean that spelling is unimportant; it is a tool which children need to learn to use to the best of their ability.

The ability to become a good speller is not a matter of memorising word lists, but rather of growing linguistic knowledge and the acquisition of various useful strategies. Some children are able to develop these strategies apparently unaided, while others will not become competent unless they are rationally and systematically taught.

Children go through stages of exploring different ways of spelling in order to gain command over words, just as they did when they learned to speak.

As children develop letter knowledge, they begin to incorporate it into their writing. With growing linguistic awareness, children become more confident and their spelling begins to replicate real words.

As their ability to write grows, the shift from oral to visual memory takes place. Children begin to check the correctness of their own responses by looking at them, not by sounding them out. Also, when they are unsure of a word, they will begin to write it out in different ways to see which way looks right. They may articulate and hear the word mentally as they write it, but the decision as to whether it is right or wrong comes from the way it looks written down.

BACKGROUND

Being a good speller makes it easier to take up your pen and write down on paper the thoughts that are buzzing around in your head. It means that you can write most of the words you need automatically, without needing to stop and think about form, structure or the order of the letters. It also means that your message can be read and understood by those for whom it is intended.

But what if you can't spell? How interesting will your message be if you're not free to concentrate on composing it? What if you do have to worry whether the reader will be able to make sense of your writing? How will you feel about yourself if you know you can't spell?

The fact that some children cannot spell does not mean that they are ignorant or incapable. Sadly, though, they often come to feel that they are, and become afraid to put pen to paper.

When we speak we don't have to think about what the words look like, but when we write we have to pay attention to things like spelling, as well as concentrating on the thoughts to be conveyed.

It is often assumed that good readers are good spellers because they are exposed to a wide range of vocabulary, but this is not necessarily so. When we read we use minimal clues to recognise words. As we become fluent we largely ignore details such as word shape, letter shape and the order of the letters and words in the text. Spelling requires the learner to notice all these things.

Sometimes phonics are used to help teach spelling, but phonics is a decoding task, in which you have to substitute sounds for written symbols. When spelling, you have to substitute symbols for sounds, often with little indication of what the symbols may be.

A direct sound-symbol relationship only works for regular words in the English language; there are many exceptions. The spelling of a word frequently does not make phonic sense. For example, there is nothing in the way one says 'laugh' to indicate whether it should be written as 'laugh' or 'larf'. It is the look of the word that confirms or rejects the spelling.

There is no one right way to teach spelling, but there are many strategies to draw upon to help children become good spellers. To use one way only may sound easy, but it is no sinecure and can become very boring for the teacher and the children. Teaching is an art, whatever the subject taught, and a varied approach with the main concepts kept constant is lively and stimulating for the children, as well as much more interesting for the teacher.

It makes us laugh!

larf

In this chapter there are suggestions for different strategies, games and ways in which we can improve the spelling competence of the children we teach. But, as with most forms of teaching, there is the added bonus that by helping children to improve their spelling we can't help but improve our own!

Which method?

It is important to establish strategies which create an effective teaching programme in your class.
• Spelling should be taught as part of the whole curriculum, encouraging children to write frequently – inventing and refining as they write.
• Children should be given spelling practice through a wide range of writing opportunities, such as labels, lists, signs, posters, cards, songs, stories, accounts, experiments, experiences, poems, letters and recipes.
• Children should be encouraged to invent words; this will make them think about words and use their knowledge about them. Concern is often expressed that if children use invented spellings, this use may become habitual. However, there is no evidence for this; it appears to be a stage through which children pass, just as they passed through the telegraphic stage of speech. Through children's misspellings and invented spellings we can see their approach to spelling and

get an idea of the stage they are at. Children learn from their mistakes, and in this way they come to understand what spelling is all about.
• Teachers should respond to children in positive ways by building up interest in words, studying words, playing with words, talking about spelling, and teaching children strategies for learning how to spell. Children need to learn to write quickly to absorb the patterning of a word and to store it in their memory. How many times can they write a word in one minute? Can they write it faster than you can?
• All children can learn how to check their work after the written task has been completed. When redrafting, teach the children to draw a wiggly line under words they are not sure of and then to check them with a dictionary. During conferencing (see page 55), talk with the children about words that were difficult and how the correct word was found, so that you know the processes each child is using, and can identify other strategies it would help the child to learn.

• Children should be encouraged to correct errors straight away, because this seems to assist their visual memory. It is important to ensure that children write the whole word from memory, not letter by letter, because this fragments the word. Children must see the word as a whole and get the flow of the word in order to store its patterns in their memory. It is this that enables them to know whether it looks right or not.

There is no one best strategy for teaching spelling. As with all learning, what works for one child may not work for another, but teachers need to have a clear understanding of what children need to learn. There should be a structured school policy on spelling which is followed by all.

Beginning formal instruction

For formal teaching on spelling to start, children need to be at the stage when they know most of the letters of the alphabet and can relate these to sounds.

NB Throughout the primary years, individual conferencing should take place alongside formal study.

How should I begin?
• First, children need to gain control of a writing implement, using a triangular grip. In order to practise this control they can colour, scribble, copy patterns, draw whirls, make shapes and shade using lines going in the same direction.
• Next, children should learn to write their own names from memory. They can write them on card and if they are long names, cut them into syllables; for example, Chris/to/pher.
• Encourage children to use letters and words in their own writing. Gradually, they will bring into use what they are learning in related language work.
• Have a word box, folder or book and encourage the children to copy words as wholes or in syllables.
• Teach the sixteen most common words (see page 62) so that writing them becomes automatic. Gradually add the others on the list. You can use photocopiable pages 158 and 159 to help with this.
• Teach the alphabet by letter names. The use of names is absolute and not open to confusion in the way that the sound can be. 'C' (see) and 'K' (kay) are not confused in the way that 'c' (cuh) and 'k' (kuh) can be.
• Later on, teach those rules which apply to a large number of words plus a few exceptions, such as that 'q' is followed by 'u'; English words don't end with 'v' or 'i' except 'taxi', 'ski', Italianate words and abbreviations; and 'k' at the end of a word is often preceded by 'c'. Teach some general rules for suffixes too, such as that 'y' changes into 'i' as in 'apply', 'applies', 'applied' and a final silent 'e' is dropped, as in 'hope', 'hoping', but a final consonant is doubled, as in 'hop', 'hopping'.

How do I choose words for learning?
• Look for the frequency of usage – oral or written – in children's language.
• Look at children's personal records of words.
• Look at your records of persistent universal or individual word difficulty.
• Analyse lists of misspellings, which should indicate word features or letter strings which need to be studied, such as:

    er or ere
    h-er-e h-ere
    th-er-e th-ere
    wh-er-e wh-ere

• Look at the one hundred most common words used in children's writing (see page 62).

The 'look, cover, visualise and write' strategy

'Look, cover, visualise and write' is a technique for learning how to spell. Children should work through the following strategy:
• see the word written correctly;
• form a correct visual image;
• identify particular features;
• associate the sound of the word with its usual image;
• see it 'behind the eyelids', thereby imprinting it in short-term memory;
• verify the correctness of the response;
• develop a means of tackling words they need or want to learn.

Look
Begin by writing the word to be learned on a strip of paper. Children need to study the features of the word carefully, because by finding out clues about the word's structure

before storing it in memory, the word is more easily remembered.

Encourage children to:
• look at the number of letters; the letters with 'sticks' (b, d, f, h, k, l, t), and the letters with 'tails' (g, j, p, q, y);
• find parts of the word that make another known word (o*ther*, *jump*er, t*went*y);
• break up words; for example, caravan into car/a/van, or today into to/day;
• make up their own clues about the word so it will have more meaning for them;
• trace over the word with their index fingers to get the feel of the word's shape.

Cover and visualise

Ask the children to close both eyes and visualise the word on the strip of paper (as if written on the inside of their eyelids). They should try to remember all the features, and then trace it on the table with the index finger.

Then ask them to open their eyes and look at the original word to check whether the word has been remembered correctly.

Write

The children should now fold the strip of paper so that the word cannot be seen and try and write it down from memory. Peeping is not allowed!

The children then check to see if their spelling of the word is correct. If it is, they should then write it three times from memory. If the word is misspelled, they (or you) tick the letters which are correct and in the correct order, to identify what is right and what is not. This way children receive reinforcement of what they do know and come to

recognise what remains to be learned.

If the word is wildly wrong, then the children start the procedure again – but it is important that you *praise* the child for the attempt already made.

This strategy helps children to gain not only a clear visual image of the word to be learned, but also a recognition of the feel of the hand's movement as it writes the word.

Children with severe spelling difficulties can be helped with order and pattern by learning to write in a joined hand. The continuous flow of writing helps the learner to associate in memory the motor movements with the words being learned.

Helping children to help themselves

Children can be helped to become competent spellers with a variety of games and skills, but by far the most important element is for the children actually to *write*. The more children write, the more likely they are to learn to spell. They need to be free to get ideas down, to try out spellings without anxiety, to write every day in a variety of genres and for a variety of real purposes, thus exploring ways of using written language just as they explored spoken language in earlier years.

They need to:
• feel at ease with words;
• be prepared to try out the spelling of a word;
• know the alphabet, its names and letter sounds;
• be able to use the 'look, cover, visualise and write' technique;
• use word collections such as dictionaries, glossaries and thesauruses with ease and confidence;
• play with words; for example, finding words within words, word families, connections, word patterns, letter strings, root words etc;
• be able to analyse what was right and what was not right in their spelling of a word, and acquire strategies to enable them to learn from a mistake.

This way children are helped to help themselves, to refine their knowledge and skills and become confident independent learners.

Essential words for children to learn

Below are listed the one hundred words which are thought to be used most frequently in children's writing. If children have command over these words it should follow that their writing content and competence are increased.

Many of the common words are also written differently from the way they sound, and are, therefore, particularly useful words for children to learn.

The words given here come from the Edwards and Gibbons list ('Words Your Children Use'); this consists of words which have been taken from children's writing. However, many of the words are also common to the Murray and McNally list ('Key Words'), which consists of words taken from children's reading books (written by adults).

The 100 words are grouped here into three lists according to frequency of usage.

• The first 16 words make up over a quarter of the words used in reading and writing. They are as follows:

a	in	of	to
and	is	that	was
he	it	the	went
I	my	then	with

• The next 24 words are:

am	had	me	some
are	has	one	there
at	have	out	they
come	her	saw	this
for	his	see	we
go	little	she	when

• The remaining 60 words are:

about	could	make	take
after	did	new	their
all	do	next	them
an	down	not	three
as	from	now	time
away	get	off	today
back	got	old	too
be	here	on	two
because	him	once	up
big	into	other	us
but	last	our	very
by	like	over	were
call	live	put	what
came	look	said	will
can	made	so	you

When choosing the words you want to teach, select those most frequently misspelled in your children's general writing.
• Don't teach words that are orally the same, but visually different or confusing like to, too, two.
• Do teach words that have similar connotations or where one forms part of the other:

is	⇒	his	⇒	this
he	⇒	here	⇒	there
our	⇒	your		
went	⇒	with		
go	⇒	for		
in	⇒	out		
look	⇒	out		

The last example in particular lends itself to cartoons. The children could practise this group of words by writing them in speech bubbles as part of a composed incident like the one shown in the illustration.

Hard spots

Drawing attention to 'hard spots' by accentuating them distorts the look of a word. It is better to give each letter its proper place and size so that the children gain the correct image of what the word looks like.

Names

Use the names of letters when helping children with spelling, because they are constant. Sounds are affected by the preceding or following letter and by the root word. To keep 'a' as '$\bar{a}$' (ay) in words like 'Sarah', 'always', 'alone', 'cake', 'want', creates less confusion in the child's mind.

Over-articulate

In speech we often gloss over syllables in words such as 'gov'nment', 'lib'ry', 'temp'rature'. It is, therefore, often helpful to teach children to over-articulate these 'lost' parts of words when spelling them – 'gov/ern/ment', 'li/bra/ry', 'tem/per/a/ture'.

Hyphens

Using hyphens to divide words into syllables distorts the word shape. Children who have a good working knowledge of the language can cope with them, but it is not helpful for most others, especially beginners.

ACTIVITIES

1. Daily five

Age range
All ages.
Group size
Individuals or small groups.
What you need
Zigzag books or word books.
What to do
Try to have a five-minute session every day to learn essential and useful words, rather than having one long lesson once a week. This seems to increase the speed and quantity of words learned by the children. For example, six- to seven-year-olds can usually manage to learn to spell three simple words a day, eight- to nine-year-olds can learn four, ten- to eleven-year-olds five and twelve- to thirteen-year-olds six words each day.

Choose words that are visually similar and take them from either the one hundred common words list (see page 62) or current classroom work.

Write the words to be learned in front of the children, and talk about the common features of the words, including the ascenders and descenders, the number of syllables, and so on.

Use the 'look, cover, visualise and write' strategy with the children. Encourage them to practise the new word by writing, drawing, painting and modelling. They can write the word in sand, PVA adhesive or paint, make the word in dough and bake it or leave it to harden, or write it with a candle or wax crayon and cover it with a colour wash.

Whenever they have a spare minute, encourage children to practise their new words using different media. The words must be written from memory rather than letter by letter.

2. Try it again

Age range
All ages.
Group size
Individuals or small groups.
What you need
Zigzag strips (see photocopiable page 160).

What to do
Give each of the children a zigzag strip which they should fold in four. They can then copy the word they wish to learn into the first column, or you can write it for them.

The children should then use the 'look, cover, visualise and write' strategy on the 'try it here' sections.

Having learned the word, the children should copy it from memory into their own 'Words I know' books, checking that it has been remembered correctly! The strips can then go home for the children to share the success of their attempts with their families.

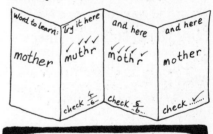

3. Flap wallets

Age range
Six to eleven.
Group size
Individuals.
What you need
Card, fabric, strong polythene (A5 size), strips of card about 2cm narrower than A5.
What to do
Staple the card, polythene and fabric together, in that order, on one long side. Staple only the card and polythene on the other long edge.

Have a number of cards cut so that they fit under the polythene, and write on them the words a child wishes to learn. As soon as they are able, let the children themselves write the words they need.

The child can then slide the word to be learned into the pocket between the card and the polythene. To use the wallet the child lifts the fabric and studies the word, its ascenders, descenders, number of letters etc, then drops the flap and writes the word from memory. To check the accuracy of her response the child can lift the flap.

If she gets stuck she can lift the flap for a sneaky look, but she should soon be able to write the word from memory after only one look.

If the child has difficulty moving from copying to writing from memory, start with short, easy words and gradually build up to longer and more complicated ones as she gains confidence.
Further activities
You can choose common words for the wallets or topic words that you've noticed children get wrong.

4. Alphabet order: 1

Age range
Five to seven.
Group size
Individuals.
What you need
Photocopiable pages 161 and 162, dot-to-dot books.
What to do
Use photocopiable pages 161 and 162, or choose attractive but simple pictures from dot-to-dot books and trace over any printed lines, replacing the numbers with the letters of the alphabet, in the correct order.

Photocopy your master so that the children can link the letters in the correct sequence to discover the picture. A recognisable finished shape of an animal, vehicle or toy helps children to know if they have linked the alphabet correctly.

It is important to make as much of the work as possible self-correcting. This allows children to check for themselves, to start making judgements about why they have made errors and to learn to work out what they should have done.

5. Alphabet order: 2

Age range
Five to seven.
Group size
Two to four players.
What you need
52 plain playing cards, each marked with a letter to make two complete alphabets. Use only one colour so the two sets are interchangeable.
What to do
Each player is dealt seven cards, and the next card is laid on the table, while the rest of the pack is kept face down in a stack. The player on the right of the dealer starts the game by laying down, in alphabetical order, as many cards from his hand as he can, on either side of the dealt letter, to make up a correct alphabetical sequence. When he has laid down all the cards he can, he replaces them by taking the same number of cards from the top of the pack. If he cannot go he should select a card from his hand to start another alphabet. It is important that children say the name of each letter as they play them.

If any of the players cannot go they can put two cards at the bottom of the pack and take two off the top as their turn.

The game can also be played from 'A' forwards or from 'Z' backwards.

As with any work children undertake, the task should help them to learn what they need to know, strengthen a weakness or reinforce new learning, otherwise it is a waste of time!

6. Letter hunt: 1

Age range
Five to seven.
Group size
Small groups.
What you need
Large sheets of paper (A1 or larger), various magazines, mail-order catalogues, newspapers, sweet wrappers, clean food packaging, cereal boxes, PVA adhesive.
What to do
Draw the outline of something that begins with a letter you are working on, such as a large bus for the letter 'b'.

The children should then cut out pictures or words that begin with the letter from the magazines and other sources, and build up a large collage on the shape. Contributions can be sought from home, thus encouraging parental co-operation. By including a wide variety of representations of the letter, children come to understand that each letter's basic form can have many variations of size, shape, colour and style.

Pin a copy of the letter on the outside of your classroom door, or send a note home to parents so that they can reinforce 'this week's letter'. Most children will be able to write home, even if it is only to say, 'Mum, b', to inform their parents of the chosen letter. This in itself gives purpose to the writing task.

An alphabet strip with a frame that slides along the strip is helpful in the classroom, as it draws attention not only to the letter itself but also to its place in the alphabet.

7. Letter hunt: 2

Age range
Five to seven.
Group size
Individuals.
What you need
Sheets of A4 paper mounted on card, hole puncher, thin cord or string, plastic cup-hook or similar.
What to do
Make a chart to display the letter which the children are learning by hanging the

mounted sheet of paper from a hook using a piece of string or cord.

The children should then write on the chart, from memory, words which begin with that letter. Spelling requires children to write from memory, so we must encourage children to do so when they are working from what they know.

Often the list will include the children's names and those of their friends or family. Use these as an opportunity to talk with the children about the use of capital and lower case letters.

8. Newspaper search

Age range
Five to seven.
Group size
Individuals, pairs or small groups.
What you need
Newspaper, highlighter pens, timer.
What to do
Agree with the children what they are going to try to find in the newspaper – a common word, a single letter, a letter string – and how much time they are allowed for the task.

Ask the children to set the timer and see how many instances of the word or letter string they can highlight in the time agreed.

Pairs or groups can search for the same word and compare totals at the end of the agreed time. Words like 'and' and 'the' build up high totals very quickly! Children can also work in supportive pairs. This game is a good one for children to take home and share with their parents.

9. Pelmanism pairs

Age range
Five to eleven.
Group size
Two to four.
What you need
Two copies of ten common or topic words written on plain playing cards.
What to do
The cards are placed face down on the table. The first child turns over one card and says the word. She then turns over another and says that word. If the words match, she keeps them and has another go; if they do not match, she turns them over and replaces them

in their original positions, and the next child has a go. The child with the most pairs wins the game.

It is a good idea to start by using the most common words, as this will help the children to learn these useful words.

This activity does not require teacher intervention and is seen by children as a game. It can be played for many years, using words of increasing complexity and allowing each group of children to work at the appropriate level.

10. Bingo

Age range
Six to eleven.
Group size
Small groups.
What you need
One base card like the one shown below for each child, sets of call cards.

can	see	it
when	lost	to
do	like	as
and	for	in

What to do
The children can play this game once they have a reading vocabulary of ten words. You can have several sets of cards

according to the range of needs in your class, perhaps choosing common words or words which reinforce letter strings, prefixes or suffixes.

The words are read aloud twice by the caller, and the first to find the word on his card covers it with the called card. Each child takes it in turns to be the caller, and so everyone has the opportunity to read the words out loud.

Children enjoy playing this game, which gives them plenty of opportunity to reinforce known words and helps with sorting and discriminating.

11. Cut and make

Age range
Six to eleven.
Group size
Individuals or pairs.
What you need
Short strips of paper and felt-tipped pens.
What to do
Write on the strips of paper words which contain other words or letter strings you would like the children to learn, like 'the' or 'and'. Use

groups of words such as 'other', 'another', 'mother', 'father', or 'land', 'sandy', 'stand', 'bandage'. The children then cut up the letter string and remake the words several times before sticking the complete word in their books.

When they have finished, ask them to close their books and write the word they had to find from memory.
Further activity
Use words which, when cut up, make two or more complete words. The children can then cut them up to make two words from one, such as 'in/to', 'car/pet', 'butter/fly'.

After the children have cut up and made two words from one and one word from two several times, they can remake them and stick them in their books.

When they have finished you can see how many words they can write from memory.

13. Word masters

Age range
Six to eleven.
Group size
Individuals or pairs.
What you need
Photocopiable page 163.
What to do
Use photocopiable page 163 and enter in the rectangles the word or letter string which you would like the children to master. Put the prefix or suffix letters in columns one and two, as shown below.

The children then make up the words and enter them in column three. Using the 'look, cover, visualise and write' technique the children should fold under the first three columns and write the completed words from memory in column four.

between them, for example 'can/not', and 'rab/bit', to prevent them writing 'canot' and 'rabit'.
Further activities
The children can repeat the activity using words they want to learn.

12. Seeking syllables

Age range
Six to eleven.
Group size
Individuals or pairs.
What you need
Strips of paper with two- to three-syllable words written on them.
What to do
The children say the word that is written on a strip of paper, and then cut it up into discrete segments. If the cut pieces form known words, such as 'car/a/van', this is much more helpful to the learner. If the word has a double consonant it helps the children if it is cut

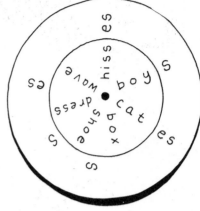

fill in the spaces with other letters. Photocopy the page for each child to complete.

14. Letter group search

Age range
Six to eleven.
Group size
Pairs or small groups.
What you need
Photocopiable page 164.
What to do
Write on to a copy of photocopiable page 164 the letter group you would like the children to work on, and the letters that have to be added to make complete words.

Enter the words created on to the word-search grid, and

15. Word wheels

Age range
Six to eleven.
Group size
Individuals or pairs.
What you need
Two cardboard circles, one at least 3cm larger than the other (see photocopiable page 165), brass fasteners.
What to do
Using photocopiable page 165 as a guideline, cut out the circles and assemble them by putting the smaller card circle on top of the larger one. Fasten them together by pushing a

paper-fastener through the centres of the circles. Fill in the circles as shown in the illustration, with initial letters, letter strings or final letters of words on the outer circle and endings or beginnings of words on the inner circle. You can either use the examples given on the photocopiable page, or fill in the blank circles with words of your choice.

The children should then use the wheels to make as many words as they can, and write them down.
Further activities
Use the wheels to examine:
• plurals – -s, -es, -ies;
• silent letters;
• prefixes or suffixes.

16. Shannon's game

Age range
Six to eleven.
Group size
Pairs or small groups.
What you need
Paper, pencil, counters.
What to do
Mark on a piece of paper a row of dashes, one to represent each letter in a word. To start with, mark in the initial letter of the word – later on this can be left out. Give the children a clue to the word's meaning or usage.

They can then take it in turns to guess the next letter. When somebody makes a correct guess he or she earns a counter, and the letter is written in its space.

When it is their turn to guess the children may also attempt to guess the whole word, if they like, before trying the next letter. Whoever guesses the whole word correctly earns three bonus counters.

17. Word chains

Age range
Six to eleven.
Group size
Pairs or small groups.
What you need
Paper, pencil.
What to do
Ask the children to change one word into another in an agreed number of steps, changing only one letter at a time. For example, they could try to change the word 'had' into the word 'men' in three steps, as follows:

had
mad
man
men

18. Growing words

Age range
Six to eleven.
Group size
Pairs or small groups.
What you need
Paper, pencil, counters.
What to do
These games are based on single letters or letter strings. Younger children will work best with an adult or older child who chooses the initial word. Older children can take it in turns to choose the starter word, or the winner can choose the next starter word.

Game 1
Start with words of three or four letters and increase the number of letters as children become more confident. They should make word chains by taking the last letter of the first word to start the next word:

wink
king
girl
loop...

Game 2
The children write down a short word. This time the next word in the chain begins with any letter of the first word, but must include all the remaining letters in the correct order:

big
igloo
loot
otter
tern...

Younger children can be encouraged to use a dictionary to find new words. In so doing they will be refining their dictionary skills, finding patterns in words, looking at differences and widening their knowledge of words.

19. Using spelling lists

Age range
Seven to eleven.
Group size
The whole class.
What you need
A spelling book for each child approximately 8cm by 20cm.
What to do
Children learn best if the words to be learned have meaning for them. But how can teachers select words for children to learn on an individual basis when working with a class full of children?

Using the spelling book, fold the page in half lengthways. During each week the children should list in their books words that they use quite often but frequently get wrong, or words that they want to know how to spell. They must look up the word in the dictionary to make sure that it is copied correctly.

The list of words (15 or 20, depending on the age and ability of the children), can be collected one week, learned the following week and then tested.

During the test, the children should fold under the half of the page which has on it the list of words they have been learning. As quickly as possible, they should then try to write out the list of words from memory.

They can then open out the original list and check what they have written. This

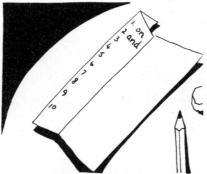

checking is best done by the children themselves; in this way they will be able to see where they have made a mistake.

Any word that a child has got wrong should go forward to join the list of words for next week, and can then be

practised using the 'look, cover, visualise and write' technique (see page 60).

Any teacher-testing should be based on the common words children have already learned. Testing should always reinforce this learning, enabling children to write the newly acquired words both automatically and speedily, and the whole process should take away any feeling of stress, replacing it with a sense of fun and success.

If children are given a chance to learn words that matter to them, and ones which they will need in their own writing, they will be freed to write more easily and fluently.

20. Word hunts

Age range
Seven to eleven.
Group size
Large groups or the whole class.
What you need
A strip of paper clipped to thick card and pinned to the wall.
What to do
Select a letter string that is useful and appropriate for the children and write it at the top of the list.

Every time the children come across a word containing that string, they should write it on the list. This way the patterning of words is highlighted, and attention is drawn to the fact that words may look the same but they do not always sound the same. For example, using the string 'one' we find words like al*one*, d*one*, g*one*, hon*e*st, hon*e*y, lon*e*ly, sh*one* and st*one*.

It is important to remember that it is the look of the word that confirms whether it is right or not, not the sound, and word hunting allows children to concentrate on looking at how words are made up.

21. Strings and things

Age range
Seven to eleven.
Group size
Pairs or small groups.
What you need
A set of cards with letter strings on them.
What to do
Give each child a card with a letter string on it. The first child to write ten words containing the letter string is the winner.

22. Compound pairs

Age range
Seven to eleven.
Group size
Two to four.
What you need
Two sets of blank cards and felt-tipped pens.
What to do
Write on one set of cards some words which can be the start of longer words, like 'camp', 'love' and 'help'. Mark or stamp the backs with a coloured shape. On the second set of cards write the endings, like '-ing', '-ed', '-ly'. Mark the backs of these cards with another shape of a different colour. The cards are then placed face down on the table in their packs.

The children should take it in turns to pick up one card from each pack and attempt to make a complete word. If they are successful they have another go; if not, then they must return the cards to the bottom of the right pack and the next player has a go. The winner is the one who has the most pairs once all the cards are gone.
Further activity
Have prefixes like 'un', 'pre-', 'dis-', in one set and words like 'even', 'fix', 'obey', in the other.

23. Dictionary game: 1

Age range
Seven to eleven.
Group size
Small groups or the whole class.
What you need
Dictionary, tokens.
What to do
Ask the children to open their dictionaries in the middle; invariably it will be at the letter 'M'. Then they should divide the first half in two again (they will usually find the letter 'D'). Dividing the second half usually finds the letter 'S'.

As children learn to find these location points they more readily find the sections for the letters in between.

Award points or tokens to the children who find the sections first. Used as a team game this speeds up children's ability to find their way around a dictionary and the alphabet.

24. Dictionary game: 2

Age range
Seven to eleven.
Group size
Pairs, small groups or the whole class.
What you need
Dictionary, tokens, sets of ten letter cards in envelopes, a pencil, two strips of paper per child (one long enough to write out the alphabet, the other with space for ten numbers and ten words).
What to do
Give each group one envelope. Ask the children to write out the alphabet on the longer strips and numbers from one to ten on the shorter ones.

The first child should then take a card from the envelope, put it face up on the table and say 'go'. The rest of the children then must search in their dictionaries for a word starting with that letter. If they are unsure where the letter comes, they can refer to their alphabet strips. The first child to find a word gets three tokens, the second two and the third one. The children then copy their own words correctly against the number one on their number strips.

Another child then takes a letter and the searching process is repeated. After ten 'goes', the child who has the most tokens is declared the winner.

Players quickly learn alphabetical order and become familiar with using a dictionary through this simple but involving game, and fast or slow players can be paired with others of like ability.
Further activity
• Once this game is mastered others can be devised, using initial letter strings consisting first of two and then of three letters.
• Words can be used instead of letters, but the words must be within the children's knowledge; they can be part of current topic or class work. This game is played in the same way as the letter game, except that the caller says the word and then turns the card face down. After the word has been found in the dictionary, the card is turned over.
• For older or more able children, use trick starts such as knee, pneumatic or gnaw ('n'

sounds); rhubarb or wreck ('r' sounds); chronicle or kimono ('c' sounds); cygnet or psyche ('s' sounds).

25. Homophones

Age range
Seven to eleven.
Group size
Individuals or small groups.
What you need
A set of cards with homophones written on them.
What to do
Homophones are words which sound the same but have different meanings ('homo' meaning 'the same', and 'phone' meaning 'sound').

With the set of cards the children can play Pelmanism, snap, dominoes and other games. For a list of common homophones, see photocopiable page 186.

26. Plus or minus

Age range
Seven to eleven.
Group size
Individuals, pairs or small groups.
What you need
Paper, photocopiable page 166, pencils.
What to do
Using photocopiable page 166, insert the letter string you want the children to work with, and supply the starter word. The children then change one letter each time, as shown above, and indicate whether they have added a letter (+ 1), taken one away (–1) or exchanged one (× 1). Each word may only be used once.

27. Word-search

Age range
Seven to eleven.
Group size:
Individuals.
What you need
Photocopiable page 167, pencils.
What to do
Make a list of common words, topic words, word patterns, seasonal words, words from stories etc. Write the list either at the bottom or to one side of the grid. Fill in the base grid with the words on the list. At first, write words from left to right and top to bottom to avoid confusion or reversals. As children become more confident word-users, fill in the words in the normal word-search manner, that is with some words backwards, some up and some down, some diagonally from left to right, up or down, and some from right to left, up or down.

Fill in the spaces with parts of the words used so children really have to search for the words on the list. Name the sheet according to the content of the list. Photocopy one finished sheet per child and explain to children the way the words have been entered and what they have to do. Suggest that they rule a line through each word that they find on the grid and cross them off the list.

Further activities
Use three-, four- or five-lettered well-known words for the youngest children. Older pupils take great delight in making word-searches for younger children and for their peers.

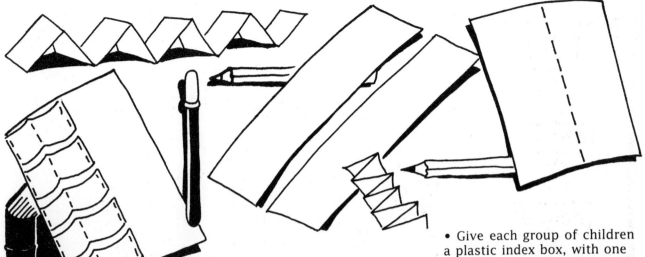

28. Word stores

Age range
Five to eleven.
Group size
Individuals or small groups.
What you need
Stiff card, cartridge paper, index boxes, index cards, storage pockets, felt-tipped pens, adhesive, staples, dictionaries, thesauruses, encyclopaedias, alphabet books.
What to do
Children need to be as independent as possible if they are to make real progress with their writing. One way is to give them access to a wide variety of words stored in a system that makes for easy retrieval.

When using any of the word store ideas outlined below, children should write out the word they want in rough first before searching it out. Then having found the word they can check the correctness of their initial spelling. They should tick the letters that are in the right order. This way they reinforce what was correct about their attempt and can see what they need to learn. Some children like to have a word book in which they can store words that are important to them.

Having checked the word, they should use the 'look, cover, visualise and write' technique to write the word from memory.

• Make a word collection, using topic words, common words or words the children find difficult. Take a piece of stiff card and mark it into two columns. Then take two strips of cartridge paper twice the length of the card but half the width, and fold them concertina-wise to make pockets, as shown. Staple the pockets at either end and in the middle, to make each pocket into two, and into each one slip a little card on which one of the words on your list is written. Write the word on the outside of the pocket too, and hang the word collection where children can reach it.

• Give each group of children a plastic index box, with one card for each letter of the alphabet, and one for each of the digraphs 'ch', 'sh', 'th' and 'wh'. Start off the word store by writing on each card some words suggested by the children, and as further words are needed they can be added. If the children add words of their own, ask them to check the spelling *very carefully* in a dictionary first. Looking up words and putting the cards back in the correct sequence will reinforce children's knowledge of alphabet order.

• On large sheets of card, keep alphabetical lists of common difficult words, topic words, word families, word patterns, unusual words and words you would like the children to learn. Don't leave any of these up for too long, or display too many at once, or they will become like wallpaper.

• Encourage the children to use dictionaries, glossaries, thesauruses, alphabet books, encyclopaedias and word lists to look up the words they need. Show them how to find a word by looking at its first, second and third letters to establish its place in alphabetical order.

CHAPTER 5

Handwriting

Being able to write easily, speedily and legibly has a profound effect upon the quality of the content of written work. It means that you can write your ideas down on paper before they slide out of your mind, and can return to them later to redraft and edit your work.

Good handwriting which is well presented is also much more persuasive than untidy work, written in an ill-formed hand. The perception others have of your competence to express yourself is often formed more from the look of your work than from what you have written.

The speed and clarity of your writing also affects your ability to become a good speller.

Handwriting is, therefore, an important life skill. It is also a craft and, like all other crafts, it has to be learned.

Most children, irrespective of academic ability, can learn to develop an easy, readable style, but if they are left to their own devices they are unlikely to do so.

There is no magic formula for developing a good style of handwriting. It is the outcome of consistent, structured teaching through the primary years, and depends on the setting of a good example.

Each school must have a style which is taught consistently and used by staff and children alike. Children's writing is unlikely to be better than the example placed before them. Consequently, when writing for children, in their books, on the blackboard or for display purposes, a teacher's handwriting must be the best possible example of what the children are striving for, so that correct images are constantly being reinforced.

BACKGROUND

Handwriting can only be effectively taught by practising a good basic style from which a mature hand can develop. It is essentially a movement exercise, which quickly becomes automatic, so it is important that the correct shape is learned from the beginning.

When teaching handwriting, as opposed to encouraging emergent creative writing, it is best to work in small groups where children can be carefully taught and watched to ensure that the letters are formed correctly. Sending beginners away to copy the teacher's writing will not guarantee that the correct movements are being made.

It is important not to have a radical change of shape when moving from print to a joined style of writing. Changing the look of a word can cause confusion which may well have repercussions for spelling.

What are children able to do?

Children should be able to:
• produce upper and lower case letters in a consistent legible style, with properly orientated ascenders and descenders;
• progress to a clear, legible joined style of writing without having to think about it;
• produce clear handwriting in both print and joined styles which can be adapted for a wide range of purposes;
• present work in a form appropriate to the task, so that the finished product is suitably and attractively presented.

The three Ps – pen, paper, position

Pens and pencils, paper and the positions that children adopt when writing are all contributory factors to developing a good style of writing. It is, therefore, important to examine:
• the way a child holds the writing tool;
• the tool that is being used;
• the way the paper is placed;
• the height of the child's chair relative to the table.

Pens and pencils
From the very start, a constant watch should be kept to see that children hold their writing implement with a triangular grip, in a relaxed hand which rests, with the forearm, lightly on the surface of the table. If a child has poor fine motor skills, a rubber triangular grip fitted over the child's pencil helps enormously.

The writing implement should be held approximately 2cm from its point and at an angle of 45° from the paper. The shaft must be thick enough for children to hold.

A wide variety of writing implements should be available, including pencils, felt-tipped pens, fountain pens and pen-holders with steel nibs of different widths.

Paper
The paper should be placed to the right of the body's midline, turned slightly to the left if the child is right-handed and to the right if the child is left-handed. It should be far enough from the edge of the table for the forearm to rest on the table.

Position
The height of the tables and chairs should be correct for the age and size of the pupils. Recommended sizes are shown in the chart below. This allows the child's feet to be flat on the ground, gives sufficient leg room and allows space for the forearm to rest on the table.

The child should be able to sit with a straight back, leaning slightly forward. Sprawlers do not have the necessary control over the pencil or the paper, and so poor writing and bad formation habits creep in.

Check that strong sunlight or artificial light does not reflect off the paper into the children's eyes, that their body positions do not cast a dark shadow over their paper and that the light does not reflect off the blackboard so that it prevents the child from seeing the writing on it.

Age of pupils	Height of table	Height of chair
5-7 years	550mm	320mm
7-9 years	600mm	355mm
9-11 years	650mm	390mm

ACTIVITIES

1. A writing corner

Age range
Five to eleven.

Group size
Individuals or groups of three or four.

What you need
A couple of tables, chairs, lined and unlined paper and a variety of suitable writing implements.

What to do
Make sure that the writing corner is freely available for use, and encourage the children to use it frequently throughout the day.

Tell them that the writing corner is a place where they can practise their writing, and then leave them free to write.

Provide letter cards, name cards, display charts and posters with examples of the school's writing style on them.

If you have a reluctant user or a child whose fine motor control is poor, suggest a number of useful purposes for writing, such as taking down a message for you and giving it to another teacher.

Children need the opportunity to write with a wide range of implements such as thick and thin crayons, chunky and normal pencils, marker pens, felt-tipped pens, chalks, pastels and charcoal. They should have a chance to work on paper of different types and shapes, including thick card, white boards and chalk boards. This way they will be able to explore making marks in a variety of different mediums.

Older children need access to ink and dip pens with a variety of nibs, and chisel- or wedge-shaped carpenter's pencils. A typewriter and, if possible, a word processor are valuable additions. Facilities for mounting finished work should also be available close by.

Even before children have learned to read, encourage them to 'read' back what they have written to someone else. Ask that person to respond with a written message of their own, to reinforce the fact that writing is about giving and receiving messages of one kind or another.

Put up a cork board in the corner, and provide a supply of pins for children to display their messages.

2. Places for writing

Age range
Four to six.
What you need
Home-made note-pads and pencils.
What to do
Place the note-pads and pencils wherever there is the remotest chance of their being used – in the shop, in the home corner, by the telephone, in the library corner. Encourage children to write messages as a result of their activity and to leave notes for each other.

3. Scribbling to write

Age range
Four to six.
Group size
Individuals.
What you need
Various implements and writing surfaces.
What to do
From the day they start school, encourage the children to write messages to each other, to you and to others. The messages may only be scribble, but this can tell you a lot about a child's readiness to write.

By looking at the notes, you will discover whether the child equates letter shapes with writing. You will find out whether the child understands that writing forms lines across the page, going from left to right and from top to bottom.

Give praise for everything that is written, but be specific. Say what it is that you like about it, whether it is the things already mentioned or just that they have written a message for you.

Ask them to 'read' to you what they have written and, with your finger, point to the place where the writing should start. Trace under their writing as they 'read' it back to you. If the children can do this for themselves you have learned what they know about writing, and whether they are ready to make sense of learning to write letter shapes.

The more you talk with children about their scribble writing, praising the beginnings of directionality and letter shape, the more it will be evident in the children's work. This, alongside the development of detailed drawing, will lead children to 'proper' writing.

4. Drawing to write

Age range
Four to six.
Group size
Individuals.
What you need
A variety of drawing tools and surfaces.
What to do
Most children are eager to draw pictures with or without being asked, and through drawing they acquire lots of skills which are essential to good handwriting.

Show them how to hold their drawing implement correctly, that is in the triangular grip. This learning will be transferred when they come to use pens and pencils for writing.

Encourage children to concentrate on what they are doing when they are drawing. If their attention flags, let them go off and do something else, but encourage them to come back later to add to what they have already drawn.

Ask them to tell you the story of their picture, and help them to think about how they can extend it, alter it or add to it. Of course, this is also the beginning of composing, but the ability to draw shapes within shapes indicates the level of motor control and, therefore, a child's readiness to learn to shape letters.

Children are usually ready to learn to shape letters when their drawings show a person with arms and legs in the right places, giving some indications of fingers and feet, and including shapes within shapes such as eyes with pupils or buttons on clothing.

5. Beginning

Age range
Five to six.
Group size
Individuals.
What you need
A variety of writing implements and different textured papers.
What to do
Handwriting is not a difficult skill to master. It is a low-level activity and well within the compass of the majority of children but, like so many things, it is how it is taught in the beginning that determines how well it is learned.

To begin with, children need to experiment with writing implements and surfaces to find out what they can do with them, and to help develop their fine motor muscles. They need to scribble, draw and colour freely inside lines, on lines and between lines.

From these scribbles you can see whether the children are merely scribbling or beginning to make pattern shapes. Do they replicate shapes needed for writing? Are the scribbles zigzag, up and down, left to right, top to bottom, circular, clockwise or anticlockwise?

Can the children draw straight lines, use continuous, flowing patterns, draw a recognisable picture? If so, they are ready to start to learn to write letters. If they cannot, then they need more opportunity for free drawing – much more. Other activities should include drawing lines from one object to another, drawing lines between pairs of straight and later curved lines, tracing paths through mazes, colouring, cutting out. Working with clay, Plasticine, constructional toys, jigsaws, paint and paste also helps to develop fine motor control.

When children are starting to form letters, work with a small group at a time so that you can watch carefully to make certain that the letters are started in the right place and correctly formed. Left to their own devices children will not make the letters correctly, and sending them away to copy your writing will teach them nothing of value. It is better for them to spend five minutes a day working hard with you and a lot of time making patterns, drawing, and creating their stories in pictures than to spend half an hour vainly attempting to write on top of or underneath your writing.

At this beginning stage you cannot expect children to cope with making their letters

correctly and composing what they want to say without something being lost, so treat these skills as two separate activities. Stimulate the development of fine motor control and encourage children to draw free-flowing patterns and letter shapes. This should take place separately from, but alongside, the development of composing through picture-making. You will soon find that the letters learned merge with and become an integral part of the story being drawn.

6. Letter recognition

Age range
Five to seven.
Group size
Individual or small groups.
What you need
Pieces of felt, velvet, flock wallpaper, plastic and other textured materials, pale backing sheets and card (both A5 size), a chalk board or white board, thirty-second timer.
What to do
Cut out letter shapes from different textured fabrics or paper, and mount them on

backing sheets and then on to card. Initially, make a set of lower case letters only.

Place a green dot with an arrow at the place where the children should begin to write the letter, and a red arrow leading to a dot where they should stop.

The children can trace over the letter shapes with their index fingers to develop the motor movement of the letter shape. After doing this several times they can draw the shape on a white board or a chalk board.

Once children have learned how to write the letter, ask them to guess how many times they can write it and rub it out in the space of 30 seconds. A friend can do the timing for them so they can concentrate on writing the letter. This way the outline of the letter shape is stored in the memory.

7. Letter shapes

Age range
Five to seven.

Group size
Individuals or small groups.

What you need
Pencils or felt-tipped pens, unlined paper, cards of letter patterns and shapes (see photocopiable pages 168 to 171).

What to do
Print script tends to be fairly straight, and many shapes end abruptly, which prevents the development of a free-flowing, fast hand. Also, when children move to a joined style, unnecessary relearning often has to take place. If joining hooks are taught as part of early letter shapes, children are led easily from their early writing to a joined style.

Make cards of letter patterns and shapes, like those shown, writing them with a thick, solid line. Show the starting point of each letter with a green dot and directional arrow, and the finishing point with a red dot. Cover the cards with clear, self-adhesive plastic.

The children can then trace the letter shape on the card with their index fingers before trying to write it as quickly as they can. Use blank paper so that the children can use free, flowing movements. Having to concentrate on using lines at this stage slows children down when they should be developing a fast hand.

Teach one basic shape, and then adapt it to other letters in the set. If you introduce letter shapes which involve similar movement patterns one after the other they are more readily learned.

Set 1 c o a d g q

Set 2 I r n m h p k

Set 3 i l b t (b instead of b avoids confusion with d.)

Set 4 v w u y j

Set 5 e f s

Set 6 x z

It seems that if children talk themselves through the writing of a letter, they learn its formation much more quickly. Merely copying the shape is not so beneficial.

In Set 1, for example, if children say 'up and round, down and round,' for the letter 'c', when they proceed to 'a' or 'd' the pencil is in the right place for the 'straight up, straight down, and put its tail on' final stroke.

In Set 2, 'down the stick, up and round the tunnel and put its tail on' is helpful for 'n' and 'm'.

In Set 5, if the beginning stroke of 's' is drawn straight there is no problem with an oversize 's'.

Wherever possible, let the children practise with real words, such as 'baa', 'cod', 'odd', 'gag', 'in', 'mini', 'rim', which can be made from one set. After all, what is the point in making children spend time learning constructions that are likely to be of no further use to them?

If children are to develop the necessary fine control needed for writing, in a reasonably short period of time, a few minutes of consistent practice every day is essential.

Further activity

Once two sets are well-established, make real words using both sets. Making real words establishes correct patterns in the children's heads, which is helpful for spelling, and also gives the writing meaning.

8. Patterns

Age range
Five to seven.
Group size
Individuals.
What you need
Shallow trays of damp sand, soft clay or Plasticine, paint and glue mixed together, a flat surface, a white board and special pens, photocopiable page 172.
What to do
Patterning is one of the best ways of encouraging the rhythmic, flowing movements essential to good, speedy writing. However, be careful, as not all patterns develop flow; in fact some even promote a cramped writing style.

The patterns which children make must relate to the movements made when writing, and should be the same size as the writing you would expect from children of that age. You can use photocopiable page 172 to start them off.

Provide the children with a shallow tray of slightly damp sand, soft Plasticine or clay, or a paint and glue mix on a flat surface for finger painting. At first, guide the child's hand as they form the letter's shape with a stick or a finger.

Another useful aid is a white board. The children can write with you or beside you or on their own. The board can be filled with patterns and shapes; its smooth surface provides no resistance to the children's efforts and encourages flow.

The left-to-right direction of English writing is encouraged by indicating the beginning with a green dot and arrow and the end with a red dot.

The patterns shown below assist the development of flow and help ensure consistency of shape and size.

No more than the equivalent of five letters should be drawn at any one time as this is the most that a hand can write without moving its position.

The following patterns do not feature in English writing and involve jerky movements. They do not help speed and

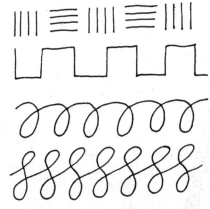

flow to develop and should not be used.

Do not be discouraged if control over the patterns and shapes takes a long time to develop; children have much to learn at this stage.

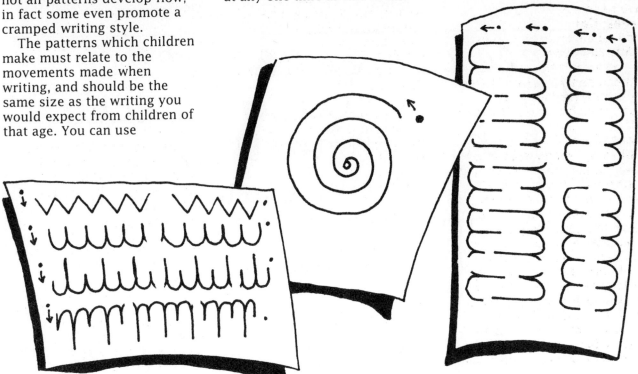

9. Ligatures

Age range
Seven to eleven.
Group size
Small groups.
What you need
Sharp pencils, lined and unlined paper, photocopiable pages 173 and 174.
What to do
A basic cursive script naturally evolves into a joined hand, which becomes a base for the adoption of a cursive or italic style in maturity.
Photocopiable pages 173 and 174 show some examples of ligatures.

Start by revising patterns learned as a novice writer. Next, introduce new ones which practise particular movements and links such as diagonal or horizontal joins, forward and back movements. These need to be taught with care, since otherwise the wrong movements will be made.

diagonal

horizontal

forward and back movements

Diagonal ligatures naturally flow from the serifs, and these tend to be the first ones taught, followed by horizontal ligatures. Use common words or letter strings that practise a particular link to increase speed and reinforce spelling patterns.

Diagonal ligatures

the in tip mum chip can ing

Horizontal ligatures

oi oy or ox box boy fox wa room wood

Once the ligatures are known, spirit-master sheets, published or home-made, can be used for practice and reinforcement. There are also computer programs designed to develop handwriting, but do check them before you use them to make sure that they conform to your school's style.

10. Calligraphy

Age range
Ten and upwards.
Group size
Individuals or small groups.
What you need
Dip pens with different width nibs, felt-tipped pens with chisel tips, fountain pens with various nibs and pen barrels, Indian ink, fountain pen ink, good quality paper, wedge-shaped carpenters' pencils, H or HB pencils and a ruler with a good straight edge.

What to do
Calligraphy gives children for whom writing has always been difficult another chance to develop a good hand. Anyone can learn to do it in a very short space of time; the teacher and pupil can learn together.

The paper should be set square to the writer, as straight letter lines are much easier to draw if the paper is straight.

The height of letters looks best when in direct proportion to the size of the nib used. A good rule of thumb is to rule the lines five stacked nib widths apart.

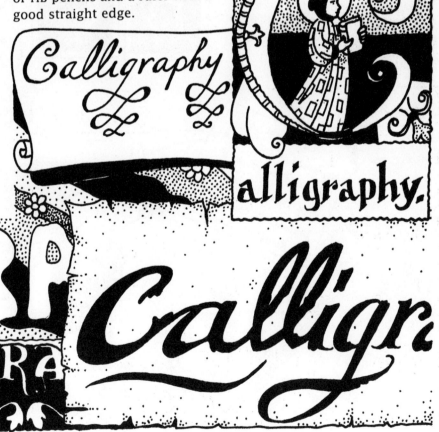

To make a straight stroke, slide the pen to the right at an angle of 30° making a short stroke to the top line (serif), then, without lifting the pen, make a thick stroke down to the writing line, finish the stroke with another serif.

For curved strokes (o), start at the eleven o'clock position and draw an anticlockwise curve round to five. Then, rejoining the pen at 11 o'clock, draw a clockwise curve from eleven to five.

Choose from one of the many good books on the market to take you on from here.

11. Presentation

Age range
Eight to eleven.
Group size
Individuals and small groups.
What you need
Presentation materials and equipment, a piece of work to be finished and presented.

What to do
Any piece of work gains immeasurably from redrafting, proof-reading and good presentation, but not all work needs it. It depends on the purpose of the writing task. From an early age children can be taught to think about the way their work looks on a page, which colour and texture of mount will enhance rather than detract from it, what title or heading it will have and how it will be written.

After the work has been redrafted for content and proof-read for spelling errors and punctuation, the children need to think about the way in which to present the writing. Audience, purpose and motor control will help to decide whether handwriting, typewriting or word processing will present it to its best advantage. Copying out a piece of work for presentation allows the child to concentrate on shaping the letters and words and gives real purpose to the task.

12. Left-handed writers

Age range
All ages.

Group size
Individuals.

What to do
The choice of which hand to use is that of the child; she will select her dominant hand for writing. Left-handed writers will be able to write just as quickly as right-handers and with equally clear handwriting.

The main sources of problems are the 'three Ps', directional flow and reversals.

Position
The writer should sit at the left of the desk to free the writing arm, and not on the right-hand side of a right-hander.

Pen
The pencil should be held in the same triangular grip as a right-hander would use but higher up the shaft. The pencil should point towards the shoulder, not away from the body.

Paper
Tilt the paper to the right so that the writer can see what she is writing.

Directional flow
Some left-handers have problems establishing left to right orientation. Young children are helped by completing tracking tasks and writing patterns which are marked green (for go) on the left, and red (for stop) on the right.

For writing activities draw a green arrow or margin on the left and a red one on the right. This guards against the 'ox-plough' effect as well as right to left writing.

If a child scans from right to left, use a mask with green (left) and red (right) markings. Provided the child is not also colour-blind, the colours act as *aides-mémoires*. After a while, drop the red marker and reduce the green to a dot. In time the green dot can also be dropped.

Reversals
In the early stages of learning to write, some left-handed children have a tendency to reverse letters, especially 'b' and 'd', which can cause confusion. This problem can be helped by the child learning to write in a joined form or by associating a little 'b' with a capital one without the top. The letter 'd' can be helped by instructing the child to 'start with "c" and then go up and down the stick'.

CHAPTER 6

Cross-curricular ideas

This chapter takes various English topics – books, poems and sayings – and shows how they can be used for cross-curricular topic work. Each of the topics is treated broadly, and they can be added to according to the needs of your pupils. They may also give you ideas for planning your own topics which fit more closely to your curriculum.

The purposes of cross-curricular topic work are manifold. Essentially, topics provide a holistic approach to learning and allow children to make connections not only between curriculum areas, but between what they already know and new knowledge they are acquiring. Topics also give children the opportunity to delve deeply into particular aspects of subjects which interest them without losing the broader curriculum elements.

Topic work 'at its best' provides an environment in which children learn, because it allows them to:
• build new knowledge and concepts on those they have already acquired;
• talk through their ideas and sort out their thinking through discussion and debate with their peers;
• apply skills already acquired in different situations;
• work co-operatively in a variety of social groups, thereby learning from each other as well as from their teachers;
• be actively involved in organising and planning their own learning;
• take responsibility for their own learning;
• reflect upon and assess their own work and progress;
• develop skills of enquiry, discovery, judgement and self-assessment.

If a topic is well planned, with resources that are clearly organised and accessible, in an environment that is stimulating and attractive, then we are providing requirements that are at the heart of good education.

Planning cross-curricular work

A topic has to be carefully planned if the children are to gain maximum benefit from it. It is a good idea to brainstorm the topic first to establish the purpose for studying it. Write down as many things as you can think of to find out about it. If you involve the children in this process then not only will they take ownership of the topic, but they may also come up with a number of things you may not have thought of!

Once you have come up with as many ideas as you can, you should transfer your thinking on to a curriculum topic web and ask yourself the following questions.
• What skills, concepts and knowledge do the children have already which will be useful?
• What new skills, concepts and knowledge will they need to acquire?

• How can the topic be designed to provide opportunities for new learning?
• What opportunities will there be for different groupings, for example, the whole class, small groups, pairs or individuals?
• What opportunities will there be for first hand experience – visitors, visits, artefacts etc?
• What parental help will be needed, and when?
• What resources will be required and where can they be obtained?
• In which ways can the information be presented?
• What will be the outcome or end product?
• Who will be the audience for the topic?

Remember, if you plan with care, the topic should run smoothly, but unplanned topics without clear objectives waste the children's time.

Presentation

Children come into contact daily with graphics of a high technical standard through television, advertisements, posters and magazines. Therefore, their own

expectation of what finished work should look like is often higher than they are capable of achieving. This means that often they are discouraged and disappointed, so it is important to provide the advice they need to help them to fulfil their expectations.

Although work can be presented through maps, plans, illustrations and diagrams, the visual quality of a page does not depend on the ability to draw. The following aspects are more important:
• attractive, uncluttered headings, handwritten or done using computer graphics;
• a high quality of handwriting or typing;
• revision and redrafting of work so that there are proper sentences, punctuation is correct and there are no missing words;
• a lack of spelling errors (any words which don't look right should be checked);
• devices which lead the reader into the work; for example, hidden data, revelation techniques, pull tabs and unfolding information;
• clear keys to diagrams;
• attractive mounting or framing, using complimenting colours.

The children can experiment with the way the work looks on the page by cutting up blocks of text and laying them out.

The following basic design points may help:
• the margin at the top of the page should be narrower than the bottom margin;
• main headings should be done in the same style;
• short paragraphs are easier to read than long ones;
• short lines look better than long ones;
• numbered items should each begin on a new line and should be placed one under the other;
• text should be placed symmetrically or asymmetrically but not randomly.

Individual project guide

Children working individually or in small groups on their own projects need to think about what they will include when writing up.

Some work will be written and some presented as diagrams or illustrations; a variety of formats helps to make a more interesting project. The following list can be used to remind children of some of the ways in which information can be presented.

Their project must have:
• an introduction saying why they chose this project and what they wanted to find out;
• a list of contents;
• a web incorporating all sorts of ideas about the project;
• a conclusion saying what they have gained from doing the project.

The children could choose from the following list some writing ideas suited to their project:
• a description of a place or item, saying what it looks like, how it feels, sounds, tastes, smells and so on;
• a newspaper report or a magazine article;
• charts and diagrams with an explanatory key;
• a write-up of an experiment;
• instructions on how to make something;
• directions to explain where to find a place or locate further information;
• a letter to someone associated with the project, real or imaginary, asking for help or advice, inviting them to

speak or visit, thanking them for their help or making a complaint;
• a personal letter;
• a postcard;
• an invitation to an exhibition of the project;
• an imaginative story;
• a poem, rhyme or jingle;
• an advert, poster or slogan;
• a pen-portrait of a famous person;
• a book review;
• a pamphlet, guide or brochure;
• a comparison of changes that have taken place over time;
• a projection into possible future developments.

Finally, the project should also have a bibliography, containing details of any reference books used.

Not all these suggestions will be right for every child's project, but the children should try to include as many ways as possible of presenting their information.

TOPICS

Books

Serialise the books for the children by reading them aloud in class every day for a short while so that the story stays fresh in their minds. You can then pick up the different tasks as appropriate for the children, and as they relate to their understanding of the story.

Speaking and listening
Ask the children to think about the following questions and activities:
• How do we know that the family intended to make the gift one of the family?
• What were their reactions when Uncle Fred mentioned the zoo?
• What is meant by 'part of the furniture'?
• What were the pros and cons of the gift?
• Re-tell a story from one of your favourite monster books.
• Dramatise a section of the story, such as the hatching sequence.

Writing
Ask the children to write:
• a letter from Winkie begging not to be sent to the zoo and giving his reasons;
• a newspaper report on the pet show or Mr Barr's mishap;
• a letter to the Natural History Museum describing Winkie and requesting information on the species;
• a piece about monsters in myths and legends, such as the Minotaur or the Loch Ness Monster;
• a story in their own words about a monster;
• a diary of the discovery and growth of Winkie, as written by Dan or Mary;
• a character study of one of the main characters;
• a poem about Winkie or one of the other characters in the story;
• a review of the book.

Handwriting
Ask the children to:
• practise diagonal links for 'ea' and 'aft' words;
• design a poster for the pet show;
• write out the poem;
• make certificates for the pet show.

A Gift from Winklesea
by Helen Cresswell (Puffin).

Spelling
Ask the children to:
• write a list of letter strings for 'ea' words;
• make a word master for 'aft' words;
• make a glossary of more difficult or unusual words;
• find out the meaning of words like 'extinct'.

Read and discuss
• *I'll Always Love You* by Hans Wilhelm (Knight).
• *Desmond the Dinosaur* by Althea (Dinosaur Books).
• *The Village Dinosaur* by Phyllis Arkle (Puffin).
• *The Lighthouse Keeper's Daughter* by R. and D. Armitage (Andre Deutsch).
• Poems from *A Fourth Poetry Book* chosen by John Foster (Oxford University Press): 'Rhamphorynchus' by Wes Magee; 'Tyrannosaurus Rex' by Wes Magee; 'Song of the Whale' by Kit Wright; 'The Walrus' by Michael Flanders.
• Poems from *Poems for Sevens and Under* chosen by Helen Nicoll (Puffin): 'Little Fish' by D. H. Lawrence and 'Baby Sardine' by Spike Milligan.

Mathematics

The children can:
- make a graph showing the pets of the children in their class;
- make an imaginative price list for items that can be bought for 40p;
- mark on the playground the lengths of different dinosaurs and compare them with everyday objects like a bus, car, lorry, house etc;
- experiment and look for patterns in doubling numbers and volumes;
- make a chart showing the effect of doubling the size of an item on the displacement of liquid in which it is placed.

Music

The children can listen to:
- *La Mer* by Debussy;
- *Ma Vlat* by Smetana;
- *Songs of the Hump-backed Whale* by Roger Payne.

RE

The children can read about:
- the crossing of the Red Sea by Moses and the tribes of Israel;
- Jonah swallowed by a whale;
- fishing on Lake Gallilee;
- the miracle of the fishes;
- the miracle of the five loaves and two fishes;
- Jesus saying 'I will make you fishers of men';
- Jesus stilling the storm;
- St Paul in the storm at sea.

History

The children can:
- find out about extinct creatures such as dinosaurs, the dodo and the Tasmanian tiger;
- list some monsters, past and present;
- research the different theories about why dinosaurs became extinct;
- create a display from a local museum study box;
- compare the seaside pleasures of Victorian times with those of today;
- discuss the reasons for changing holiday trends.

A Gift from Winklesea
by Helen Cresswell (Puffin).

Science

The children can:
- make a display of shells and pebbles;
- make a book about shells, and explain what shells can be used for;
- visit an aquarium;
- examine the differences between cold and tropical aquaria;
- study the concept of buoyancy.

Design and technology

The children can:
- design a money box for Dan or Mary;
- design and build a model of Winkie using wire netting and papier mache, wood or paper;
- design a container that will keep a model of Winkie afloat for several minutes, and then describe how this was achieved.

Geography

The children can:
- visit the Natural History Museum to study fossils;
- go fossil-hunting;
- study tides;
- list some creatures of the deep and map where they are found;
- do a mini-project on whales or other sea-creatures;
- debate the case for protecting the whales.

Art

The children can:
- make observational drawings for a book on shells;
- paint pebbles and stones as gifts;
- decorate boxes with shells as gifts;
- make a clay model of Winkie;
- design rosettes and certificates for the pet show;
- examine fossils and old bones with magnifiers and make observational drawings.

Speaking and listening
• Invite a few older people who were evacuated in the second world war to come and talk to the children.
• Topics for discussion:
Was Nicky right to stand up to Mr Evans over the ginger biscuit?
Why did Carrie change her mind about the ring?
The trauma of evacuation.
Things that frighten the children.
Relationships, motives and feelings in the story.
Is it a great handicap being a child (Albert)?
Is the title appropriate? Is it a war story? Whose war?
• Discuss the following sayings: 'You never miss the water until the well runs dry', and 'Rich people's charity can be a cold business'.

Spelling
The children can:
• list words with similar meanings;
• make an alphabetical word store of words which they don't know;
• collect from the book some phrases that explore senses, such as 'the warm starchy smell of ironing'.

Handwriting
The children can write:
• labels;
• letters home to mother in their best handwriting;
• a poem in their best handwriting.

Carrie's War
by Nina Bawden (Puffin).

Read and discuss:
• *The Owl who was Afraid of the Dark* by Jill Tomlinson (Puffin).
• 'Midnight Forest' by Judith Nicholls from her book of the same name (Faber & Faber).
• Poems from *Marbles In My Pocket* compiled by Moira Andrew (Macmillan Educational): 'Night Walk' by Max Fatchen; 'Unknown' by Leonard Clark; 'Moon thoughts' by Moira Andrew; 'Sky-silk' by L. H. Allen; 'The double' by Frances Lovell; 'Night' by Judith Nicholls.
• Poems from *Fourth Poetry Book* compiled by John Foster (Oxford University Press): 'Night without light' by Alan Bold; 'The harvest moon' by Ted Hughes.

Writing
The children can:
• draw one of the characters and label the picture using descriptive phrases from the book;
• write a pen portrait of one of the characters;
• describe what their reaction would be if they met Mr Johnny;
• say whether they think Hepzibah was a witch and give their reasons why;
• write about a frightening experience that happened to them;
• pretend to be Carrie or Nick and write a letter home to mother telling her about their new home;
• write a poem about the best gift they were ever given;
• write a further chapter to the story.

Science

The children can:
• make a display of skulls and bones, using pictures, writing, and models;
• find out what kind of bones are in the skull, and their purpose;
• find out why chickens fluff up their feathers in cold water, how they keep dry and how they keep cool;
• write down what they know about ants, and two things they would like to find out;
• find out why the ants burst into activity when Albert disturbed their nest.

Mathematics

The children can:
• Make a comparative study of prices related to wages 50 years ago and today;
• Establish percentages of food costs to wages, and map the difference.
• Find out whether money really did go further in the 'old days'.

Design and technology

Ask the children to design a machine with levers and pulleys to lift a 250g weight.

Music

The children can:
• learn wartime songs;
• find out what music and dances were popular during the Second World War.

Carrie's War
by Nina Bawden
(Puffin).

Geography

The children can:
• find Wales on a map of Britain, and identify its main towns and features;
• Draw a map to show the book's location, marking places mentioned in the story;
• find out about the mining industry in Wales and how it has changed;
• find out what effect these changes have had on the lives of local people.

Art

Ask the children to:
• make observational pencil drawings of a skull (animal, bird or human);
• paint a portrait of a character from the story;
• arrange three of the artifacts from the display and draw them in pastels or charcoal;
• paint one of the settings from the story.

History

• Display artefacts from the second world war, such as gas masks, ration books etc, and reference books about evacuation. Look at *No time to Wave Goodbye* by Ben Wicks (Bloomsbury).
• Examine and compare flat irons, gas irons, early electric irons and today's irons.

Poems

Reading
• *The Tough Princess* by M. Waddell and P. Benton (Walker Books).
• *Bike Run* by Diane Wilmer (Armada).
• Poems from *I Din Do Nuttin* by John Agard (Methuen/Mammoth): 'Duck-belly Bike'; 'All Fools' Day.
• Poems from *A Spider Bought a Bicycle*, edited by Michael Rosen (Kingfisher).

Handwriting
The children can:
• make a chart of rules for safe cycling;
• practise joined patterns using the letter 'c'.

Spelling
The children can:
• brainstorm words associated with bicycles;
• find the meaning of the prefix 'bi' and make a list of words with this prefix and their meanings.

'Esme on her bicycle' by Russel Hoban, from *Marbles in my pocket*, chosen by Moira Andrew (Macmillan Educational).

Speaking and listening
The children can:
• debate the advantages and disadvantages of bicycles versus cars;
• discuss the saying 'A chain is as strong as its weakest link'.

Writing
Ask the children to write:
• instructions for riding a bicycle, changing a tyre, repairing a puncture, looking after a bicycle or checking a bicycle for safety;
• an advertisement for the sale of a bicycle;
• letters describing a new bicycle to a friend or complaining about the bicycle to the shop where it was bought;
• a postcard sent from a cycling holiday;
• labels for a picture of a bicycle, showing all the parts;
• a poster to advertise a bicycle ride, showing the route and a list of food and drink to be taken.

Science

The children can:
- list the moving parts of a bicycle;
- find out about braking systems;
- explore the functions of wheels and gears, tyres, tubes and valves, air pressure and pumps;
- learn to repair a puncture;
- examine the function of reflectors;
- look at the durability of materials, and the causes and prevention of rust;
- find out about electrical circuits;
- learn about essential first aid for cyclists, to deal with minor injuries.

Design and technology

The children can:
- design and make a working lamp;
- design and make a warning sound, a bell, horn, or bleeper;
- make a model which moves using a gearing system.

Art

The children can:
- make pattern prints of gears and wheels;
- examine the treads of different tyres and draw, print or make rubbings of them;
- illustrate 'Esme on her bicycle' or another poem;
- draw a bicycle.

'Esme on her bicycle' by Russel Hoban, from *Marbles in my pocket*, chosen by Moira Andrew (Macmillan Educational).

Geography

The children can:
- find out why lots of people cycle in places like Holland, Singapore and Peru;
- find out the locations of major cycle races;
- find out the route of the Tour de France;
- find out about different kinds of cycle racing;
- find out about tandems, tricycles, delivery bikes, trishaws, mountain bikes and racing bikes.

History

The children can:
- find out about the clothing worn for cycling, and compare past fashions with those of the present;
- look at the development of bikes from the hobby horse to the present day;
- find out about famous people in the cycling world, past and present.

Mathematics

The children can:
- carry out a class bicycle survey;
- measure stopping distances in different weathers and at different speeds;
- make a comparative study of the cost of bicycles.

Read and discuss
- *The Secret Garden*, by F. H. Burnett (Puffin).
- *Tom's Midnight Garden*, by Philippa Pearce (Puffin).
- *The Shrinking of Treehorn*, by Florence Parry Heide (Puffin).
- The first chapters of *Alice in Wonderland* by Lewis Carroll.
- *Our Hidden Garden*, by B. Birch (Hamish Hamilton).
- *Seeds*, by T Jennings (Oxford University Press).
- *Flower Calendar*, by U. Jacobs (A & C Black).
- *The Illustrated Garden Planter*, by D. Saville (Penguin).
- *Usborne First Nature Series* (Usborne).
- *Green Finger Fun*, by Althea (Dinosaur Publications).
- Poems from the chapter on flowers in *Language in Colour* by Moira Andrew (Belair).
- Poems from *The Unicorn and Lions* chosen by Moira Andrew (Macmillan Educational): 'Flowers' by Frances Horovitz; 'Ann's flowers' by John Walsh.

Writing
The children can:
- brainstorm flower words, including their names, parts and colours;
- describe their sense impressions of flowers they like or dislike;
- write a descriptive poem about a flower;
- write haikus about flowers, their beauty, meaning, message;
- write a story about a magic garden.

'Flowers are soft', by Dave Calder, from *Language in Colour*, chosen by Moira Andrew (Belair).

Handwriting
Ask the children to:
- write poems about flowers and display them attractively;
- write the labels for a flower display.

Speaking and listening
Ask the children to describe a flower and learn the correct terminology.

Spelling
The children can:
- make letter strings for 'ee' words;
- make a word master for 'low' words;
- sort flower names into words of one, two and three syllables;
- find flower words that are made up of two words, such as bluebell, buttercup, candytuft, cowslip, foxglove, hollyhock, larkspur, primrose, snowdrop, sunflower and so on;
- list flower names used as girls' names: daisy, daphne, lily, marigold, pansy, poppy, primrose, rose, rosemary, veronica, violet, etc.

Art

The children can:
- make observational drawings of different kinds of plants, leaves and flowers;
- make leaf rubbings and prints;
- draw different kinds of gardens;
- draw, paint or create as a collage the garden from 'Mary, Mary, quite contrary', or design a metal garden or a water garden.

Mathematics

The children can:
- work out the cost of setting up a wild flower meadow in the school grounds;
- plant a sunflower and keep a diary of observations as it grows, making a graph to show its rate of growth;
- make graphs and diagrams to show the numbers of different flowers growing locally in each season.

Science

Ask the children to:
- investigate why there has been recent concern for the wild flower population;
- examine and record the different ways leaves grow from their stems;
- contrast and compare the areas of different leaf shapes.

RE

The children can:
- look at the stories about the Garden of Eden and the Garden of Gethsemane;
- make an Easter garden;
- learn and discuss the song 'Think of a world without any flowers' in *Someone's Singing Lord* (A & C Black).

'Flowers are soft', by Dave Calder, from *Language in Colour*, chosen by Moira Andrew (Belair).

Design and technology

The children can:
- design and plan a wild flower meadow for the school grounds;
- design and plan a chequerboard garden;
- design a piece of sculpture or play equipment for the school grounds.

Music

The children can:
- listen to 'Country Gardens' by Percy Granger;
- learn the songs 'English Country Garden', 'Where have all the flowers gone' and 'Mary, Mary, quite contrary'.

History

The children can:
- find out where different species of plants came from;
- study the development of gardens, for example, Tudor food-producing gardens, walled gardens, botanical gardens, physic gardens, formal gardens of the Restoration period, knot gardens, suburban gardens, the first gardening books of the early nineteenth century, and modern gardens;
- look at the work of Victorian botanists and emissaries from famous gardens;
- visit gardens such as Kew, Syon House, Compton Acres, Hampton Court, Painshill Park at Cobham.

Geography

The children can:
- make maps of the school garden, gardens they have visited or their own garden, locating fixtures and items of interest;
- study soil, testing the pH;
- research which location different plants thrive in;
- look at the effect of weather and climate upon plant growth and life-cycle.

Reading
- *Colours* from the 'First Starter' series (Macdonald).
- The 'Thomas the Tank Engine' series, by the Rev W. Awdry (Kaye & Ward).
- *Let's Paint a Rainbow* by Eric Carle (Heinemann).
- *Green Eggs and Ham* by Dr Seuss (Collins).
- *The Wizard of Oz* by L. Frank Baum (Puffin).
- *Noah Built an Ark One Day* by C. and J. Hawkins (Methuen).
- *A Pot of Gold* compiled by J. Bennett (Doubleday).
- Poems from *Language in Colour* by Moira Andrew (Belair).

Spelling
Ask the children to:
- use a dictionary and other sources to find colours beginning with as many of the letters of the alphabet as possible;
- make a letter string for 'ain';
- make a word master for 'red' words.

'The Paint Box' by E. V. Rieu, from *Language in Colour*, chosen by Moira Andrew (Belair).

Writing
The children can:
- list as many words as they can to describe different shades of a colour; for example, red, scarlet, crimson, pink, strawberry;
- write colour poems using the following starter lines: Yellow is... (metaphor poem); Red is like... (simile poem); What is green?
- write a haiku about a colour or a rainbow;
- write about the effect of colour upon mood;
- write a story on the theme of colour.

Handwriting
The children could:
- write labels for colour displays;
- write their colour poems in their best handwriting.

Speaking and Listening
The children can discuss:
- the colour of traffic lights;
- the saying 'Red sky at night, shepherd's delight';
- the colours which they feel are warm, cold, sad or happy;
- what they think the world would be like without colour;
- colour in language, for example the expressions 'in the red', 'in the black', 'a green environment', 'feeling blue'.
- what happens when they mix paints of different colours.

Mathematics
The children can:
• collect information about the colours of eyes and hair of the other children in their class, and their favourite colours, and display this information in graph form;
• draw a Venn diagram of colour mixing.

Art
The children can:
• experiment with mixing colours;
• paint pictures in three primary colours;
• paint single-colour pictures using different tones of one colour;
• make symmetrical abstracts by painting thick paint blobs and folding the paper in half;
• make observational drawings in pencil and then using coloured pencils or pastels;
• print in tonal colours, colour families, primary colours, secondary colours.

Music
The children can sing:
• 'Sing a Rainbow';
• 'Yellow Submarine';
• 'Follow the Yellow Brick Road';
• 'Greensleeves';
• 'Black is the colour of my true love's hair';

History
The children can find out about:
• William Rufus (so called because of his red hair);
• The Black Prince;
• The Black Death;
• William of Orange;
• The Wars of the Roses.

'The Paint Box' by E. V. Rieu, from *Language in Colour*, chosen by Moira Andrew (Belair).

Geography
The children can:
• identify and compare the flags of different countries;
• explore colours in space, for example, the Milky Way, a red star, a black hole etc;
• find out what happens to colours at night;
• look at seasonal colours.

Design and technology
The children can:
• design and make a stained glass window using tissue, cellophane or perspex;
• design and make coloured spectacles.

Science
Let the children
• go on a colour walk, listing all the the colours they see;
• collect specimens of minibeasts and plants, and sort them according to colour;
• blend colours with perspex sheets or colour filters;
• look at the effect of colour filters in photography;
• try to find out what colour is;
• find out why leaves are green and why they change colour;
• find out how animals use colour as a warning, or as camouflage;
• study how colours absorb and reflect light;
• look at the effects of the sun, illness, embarrassment and anger on skin colour;
• find out why rainbows appear;
• look at prisms and colour refraction.

Sayings

Speaking and listening
The children can:
• discuss the meaning of 'salt' phrases and sayings; for example, 'take it with a pinch of salt', worth his salt, old salt, salt of the earth, to salt something away, etc;
• discuss superstitions;
• look at the chants in *All the Day Through* chosen by Wes Magee (Evans).

Write
The children can:
• brainstorm a word bank;
• list words with the word 'salt' in them;
• list words that have developed from the Latin 'sal';
• write a letter to the Health Council for information on salt and health and diet;
• discuss rules for safety at the seaside.

'A pinch of salt'

Spelling
The children can:
• make letter strings for 'alt';
• make a word master for 'sea' words.

Handwriting
The children can write out and present poems, either their own or copies.

Read and discuss
• *Come away from the water, Shirley* by John Burningham (Picture Lions).
• *Captain Pugwash* by John Ryan (Puffin).
• *Master Salt the Sailor's Son* by Alan Ahlberg (Puffin).
• *A Gift from Winklesea* by Helen Cresswell (Puffin).
• *The Sea is Singing* by Rosalind Kerven (Puffin).
• *Pirates* by Colin Hawkins (Picture Lions).
• The story of Lot's wife (Genesis 19).
• 'How the elephant gets salt' by Helen Hadley, in *R & D Reading and Language Programme Level 3 Fact and Story* (Macmillan).
• 'The Sea' by Matthew Arnold, from *Poetry Allsorts 3,* chosen by Roger Mansfield (Edward Arnold).
• 'Seaside', by Jean Kenward and 'The Sea' by Lilith Norman, from *Another First Poetry Book,* chosen by John Foster (Oxford University Press).
• 'The Sea' by R. S. Thomas and 'The Song of the Whale' by Kit Wright, from *A Fourth Poetry Book,* chosen by John Foster (Oxford University Press).
• 'Until I saw the sea' by Lilian Moore, from *The First Lick of the Lolly,* chosen by Moira Andrew (Macmillan Educational).
• 'When my Dad came home from the Sea' by Ian McMillan, from *Marbles in My Pocket,* chosen by Moira Andrew (Macmillan Educational).
• 'Sea Song' from *Magic Mirror* by Judith Nicholls (Faber & Faber).
• 'Sea Fever' by John Masefield.
• 'Now the great winds shoreward flow', taken from *The Foresaken Merman* by Matthew Arnold.

Geography
The children can find out about:
• oceans and major seas;
• fresh and saltwater fish;
• the fishing industry of the United Kingdom;
• famous yacht races and their locations;
• coastal limits;
• salt marshes;
• the Dead Sea.

History
The children can:
• examine the importance of salt through history;
• find out about the derivation of the word salary;
• discover how salt was used to preserve food on board ship;
• look at a sailor's life in Nelson's time;
• find out about the unsinkable ship, the *Titanic*;
• find out about the disappearing ship, the *Marie Celeste*;
• find out how voyage times changed with the coming of steam ships.

Art
The children can:
• make a frieze or display on the topic of salt;
• make a pottery salt crock and spoon;
• listen to *La Mer* or 'Neptune' two or three times, then paint to the music.

Music
The children can:
• listen to *La Mer* by Debussy, 'Neptune' from *The Planets* by Holst, and 'Sailing' by Gavin Sutherland on the *Classic Rock* album (London Symphony Orchestra);
• sing the songs 'The Water is Wide', and 'Yellow Submarine'.

Design and technology
The children can:
• design a wave-making machine;
• find out which design of a paper boat stays afloat longest;
• design a salt box with a lid, and write instructions for making it.

'A pinch of salt'

Science
The children can:
• look at salt as a domestic cleanser, preservative, water softener and defrosting agent;
• look at the use of salt in cooking;
• look at the connection between salt and heart disease;
• find out why some animals need salt licks;
• look at the effect of salt water on plants;
• find out why it is dangerous to drink sea water;
• find out about purifying seawater;
• compare buoyancy in salt and fresh water;
• find out whether salt and fresh water have different effects on rusting.

Mathematics
The children can:
• find out the cost of salt. What makes the price vary?
• compare within a group the size of pinches of salt;
• put equal quantities of salt into hot and cold water and compare the time it takes to dissolve;
• measure the amount of salt it takes to saturate 125ml, 250ml and 500ml of water;
• compare the rates of evaporation of salt water and fresh water;
• compare the freezing points of fresh and salt water.

CHAPTER 7

English through topic work

This chapter looks at topic work as a source for English activities. Every subject, whatever the discipline, cannot help but be rich in opportunities for English, and the examples of topics given in the chapter indicate this diversity.

Cross-curricular topics are an ideal way for children to learn because they allow children to build on previous learning in a cohesive way. They provide a flexible means by which children can work at their own level, and the class can converge and diverge at different times. For example, the class can come together at the following times:
• when the theme is introduced;
• when a teaching point is being made;
• when a new concept or idea is introduced;
• when points are drawn together;
• to round off the topic.

The children can work on aspects of the topic in mixed ability groups, or individually at their own level. However, as mentioned in the previous chapter, it is important to make sure that topic work is well planned with clear objectives. Otherwise much effort can be wasted.

Key skills and concepts are important considerations when planning topic work. Each discipline has its own key concepts which open the doors to understanding, facilitate learning and provide a framework within which new learning can be assimilated. Some skills are subject-specific, but others are important for all disciplines. The skills of discussion, debate, focused listening, enquiry and research, observation, recording, spelling, handwriting and presentation are learned through a participatory process. In planning the skills and concepts which the children will learn through a topic, the teacher can provide a vehicle for this process.

Don't be afraid to tackle topic work. When planning a topic you should sort your ideas into curriculum areas, checking them against your school's policy documents and the National Curriculum guidelines to make sure that the appropriate areas are covered. Consider what you want the children to learn from the topic, make it cohesive and build on earlier learning.

When doing the detailed planning for a topic you will need to think it through fully and plan your approach, listing the areas to be covered and the skills, concepts and knowledge to be introduced or enhanced.

It is also useful to list what pupils need to know before starting the project, and any resources they may need.

Each topic will have its own fascination and, no matter what your own subject bias, if your interest is caught by a topic the children will be interested too. In this way, the end result will be satisfying to everyone.

Checklist for topic work

When devising your topic you need to plan ways in which you can develop, practise or extend language learning through a broad range of English activities. It may be helpful to bear in mind the following ideas when preparing your topic work, in order to ensure that the coverage is comprehensive.

Speaking and listening
The children should:
• listen and respond to stories, rhymes, poems, songs, pictures, television and radio programmes, computer activities, telephone conversations, discussions and collaborative planning sessions;
• speak and respond by telling stories, reciting poems and taking part in role-play;
• give and receive explanations, information, instructions and messages;
• ask and answer questions.

Reading
The children should:
• listen to stories and poems read aloud;
• read for themselves in the context of role-play, dramatic play, stories, poems and non-fiction texts;
• identify words, phrases, patterns of letters and language features;
• develop the habit of silent reading;
• read real-world language, including signs, logos, labels, menus and notices;
• interpret tabulated information;
• talk about their own reading, questioning what they read, thinking about how language is written down and assessing the content of informative text.

Writing
The children should have opportunities for:
• chronological writing in the form of diaries, stories, letters, accounts of events, accounts of tasks, records of experiences, records of observations, instructions and directions;
• non-chronological writing in the form of lists, labels, invitations, greetings cards, notices, posters, plans, diagrams, descriptions and notes;
• playing with language, making up jingles, poems, riddles and word games;
• writing stories, articles for magazines and newspapers, books, games and guides for other children;
• making books of their own experiences, guidebooks, instruction booklets, anthologies of favourite poems, cartoon stories, collections of stories for their peers and for younger children;
• writing in response to stories, poems, plays and television programmes.

Spelling
The children should have experience with:
• letter names and sounds;
• common words;
• common letter strings;
• words with regular spellings;
• word patterns;
• the 'look, visualise and write' technique.

Handwriting
The children should learn:
• basic print shapes;
• patterns for joining;
• diagonal and horizontal joins;
• a joined writing style;
• the use of different writing tools and styles;
• modelling techniques for presenting information;
• creative ways of presenting written tasks.

Information skills

The children should:
• know the alphabet;
• be able to put words in alphabetical order;
• use a dictionary, glossary or thesaurus to find out about unusual or hard words;
• use the school's library confidently to research information;
• be able to find a useful book and use it for research;
• use contents lists, indexes, headings and tables to obtain information from books;
• use skimming and scanning techniques to locate information;
• be able to make notes and then rewrite them in their own words;
• know how to present

information using a variety of modelling techniques;
• use a variety of resources to obtain detailed information on a topic.

Provision for English

The four modes of language are speaking, listening, reading (which includes study and information skills) and writing (which includes spelling, handwriting and presentation). These modes can be grouped further into audible and visible language processes and intake and output processes. Each mode is essential to learning, but all are interdependent.

Within these main areas school policy documents should include programmes of study which reflect current thinking.

Speaking and listening

Programmes of study should try to:
• develop precision, confidence and competence in speaking and listening;
• encourage children to listen to and make appropriate contributions to discussions;
• develop children's ability to suit the language they use to both audience and purpose;
• encourage children to speak audibly and with clear diction.

Reading

Programmes of study should try to:
• build on known oral language;
• encourage reading across a wide range of stimulating, imaginative literature;
• develop the ability to use reading material in the outside world;
• encourage parental participation and support.

Writing

Programmes of study for writing should try to:
• encourage writing in different contexts for a variety of audiences and a range of different purposes;
• develop a knowledge of writing in the real world and as a life skill;

• develop the ability to plan, plot and make decisions about writing;
• develop revising and redrafting skills.

Spelling
Programmes of study for spelling should try to:
• cover knowledge of common words and common spelling patterns;
• cover knowledge of the names and sounds of letters;
• teach ways of learning to spell words, including the 'look, visualise and write' technique.

Handwriting
Programmes of study for handwriting should try to :
• encourage a clear, legible joined writing style;
• allow children to write with speed and fluency;
• require children to offer attractive work using a variety of presentation techniques.

These areas of study are all presented as topic ideas later in this chapter (pages 110-124).

Information skills
Programmes of study should try to:
• develop children's research and information skills;
• introduce children to ways of finding information in books;
• encourage skimming and scanning search techniques;
• develop in children the ability to use word resource books.

Topic work and parental involvement

The three-way relationship between teachers, parents and children needs co-operation from all three parties to be successful. Usually, if parents know what teachers are doing, they will be both understanding and co-operative. It is therefore a good idea to start the academic year by arranging a 'meet the teacher' evening for the parents.

At this meeting you can share with the parents your plans for the year, your approach to learning, your expectations and your approach to discipline. Talk to them about the work your class will be doing across the curriculum and tell them about the topics you will be exploring. Many parents think that the curriculum is best taught on a subject basis, and so you may need to convince them that while some aspects of a subject discipline may

need to be taught in a discrete way, most learning benefits from the cohesive approach that comes through cross-curricular topic work.

As you tell parents about your approach to topic work and how it will cover the curriculum, explain that each project will have a different emphasis such as English, science, history or geography, but that each will fulfil both school and national guidelines.

Finally, ask for their support in the work you are planning, and discuss the kind of support you expect.

If you take this hour to meet the parents, and let them get to know you and understand what you are planning to do with and for their children, the benefits and support both you and the children will receive will last all year long.

Flight

There are plenty of opportunities to observe flight in the world around us, from flying insects and butterflies to dandelion clocks, balloons and aeroplanes. There are many first-hand experiences available too, including visits to places like the Army Air Museum at Middle Wallop in Hampshire or the RAF museum at Hendon.

Speaking and listening
The children can:
• discuss what happens when they blow dandelion clocks, spin ash or sycamore keys, make balloon rockets and fly paper aeroplanes;
• discuss the reasons why some shapes are more aerodynamic than others;
• give a talk on a famous person in the history of flight;
• listen to the story of Icarus and discuss why he failed;
• listen to and learn songs about flying.

Reading
• *The Red Balloon* by Albert Lamorisse (Unwin).
• *Meg on the Moon* by Helen Nicoll and Jan Pienkowski (Puffin).
• *Mrs Mopple's Washing Line* by Anita Hewett (Puffin).
• *Charlie and the Great Glass Elevator* by Roald Dahl (Puffin).
• *Of Time and Stars* by Arthur C. Clark (Puffin).
• *Thunder and Lightnings* by Jan Mark (Puffin).
• *The Machine Gunners* by Robert Westall (Puffin).
• *The Wind Blew* by Pat Hutchins (Puffin).
• *Peter Pan* by J. M. Barrie (Knight).
• *Blind Flight* by Hilary Milton (Hippo).
• 'The Orange Balloon' by Stanley Cook, 'twould be nice to be' by Roger McGough and 'Witch Goes Shopping' by Lilian Moore, all from *A Fourth Poetry Book*, chosen by John Foster (Oxford University Press).
• 'Butterfly' by S. T. Ansell, from *Poems for Seven and Under*, chosen by Helen Nicoll (Puffin).
• 'To a Butterfly' by William Wordsworth.

• Ask the children to read biographies of famous aviation characters, for example the Montgolfier brothers, the Wright brothers, Alcock and Brown and Amy Johnson;
• Let them research how birds and other creatures fly, and consider aerodynamics, the history of flight, hot air balloons and space missions.

Writing
The children can:
• brainstorm words associated with flight;
• make a list of things that fly;
• write a story about the travels of a balloon;
• write a poem called 'If I could fly';
• make gliders and measure the length of their flight, and then write up the experiment and display a chart of the results;
• write up the results of an experiment to see how long it takes each member of the group to blow a piece of paper a given distance;
• design and make their own kites, write about the process and discuss modifications which could be made to improve the design;
• investigate and describe how hot air balloons work;
• make notes and then write an article about how birds fly;
• study the history of flight, noting major advances and predicting future changes;
• visit a windmill and then make and label a drawing to describe how it works;
• write a newspaper report on the first landing on the moon;
• describe how bats find their way in the dark.

Spelling
The children can:
• use letter string and word masters for 'igh' and 'ly' strings and 'air' words;
• make up an alphabet of words to do with flight;
• find the other words within 'feather' and 'kingfisher', keeping letter continuity and order.

Handwriting
Ask the children to:
• write out labels for a display on the theme of flying;
• copy a favourite poem about flying into a personal anthology;
• make detailed drawings to illustrate the topic and label them neatly, adding a key if appropriate.

Information skills
The children should, where appropriate:
• know the alphabet;
• be able to put words in alphabetical order;
• use dictionaries, glossaries and thesauruses to explore unusual or difficult words;
• use the school's library confidently to research information;
• be able to make notes and rewrite them in their own words;
• know how to present information using a variety of modelling techniques;
• use a variety of resources to obtain detailed information on the topic.

Food

Children love food – its look, taste, smell and texture stimulate their imagination in such a way that they readily find words to express their thoughts and feelings about it.

Speaking and listening
The children can:
• discuss why we need food;
• talk about food additives;
• discuss the reasons for vegetarianism;
• talk about nutrition and a balanced diet;
• discuss the problems the weather creates for food production in different climates;
• invent a new food and plan a promotional presentation;
• debate whether it is the look, the taste or the smell that is most powerful in attracting us to a particular food;
• talk about the Bible stories of Pharaoh's dream and the miracle of the loaves and fishes.

Reading
The children can:
• look through anthologies for poems about food, for example the section called 'Food, Glorious Food' in *All Through The Day*, chosen by Wes Magee (Evan Bros);
• read *Germs Make Me Sick* by M. Berger and M. Hafner (A & C Black), and *Midnight is a Place* by Joan Aiken (Puffin).
• read about food-related topics such as dairy farming, wheat production and the work of Louis Pasteur and Alexander Fleming.

Writing
Ask the children to:
• brainstorm words associated with food;
• think about a favourite food and use all their senses to describe it;
• make up limericks on food;
• invent similes and metaphors to describe food;
• create advertising for a new food fad or diet;
• write warning posters and articles about a new disease called 'crispitis';
• make a chart to show which foods are fruit, vegetable, animal or cereal;
• make a Venn diagram to show which foods have fats, proteins and carbohydrates;
• list foods which are good or bad for their health;
• draw up food chains and food cycles;
• research, make notes and write about what makes a balanced diet;
• devise a week's school menus to give a balanced diet;
• write about the best or worst meal they have ever eaten;
• write a letter of thanks for a delightful meal, or complaining about a terrible meal;
• map where their five favourite foods come from;
• chew a piece of fresh bread very slowly and write about what happens to the flavour;
• write about how a favourite food is made.

Spelling
The children can:
• make an illustrated dictionary of food;
• write a food alphabet;
• use the letter string and word masters to devise word patterns based on 'food' words or letter clusters.

Handwriting
The children can:
• write labels for a visual display of food;
• copy out favourite poems about food and illustrate them;
• devise and present a menu;

• design packaging for a new food product;
• design a label for a can of drink.

Information skills

The children should, where appropriate:
• know the alphabet;
• be able to put words in alphabetical order;
• know how to use dictionaries to find difficult words;
• know how to use a thesaurus to find alternative words;
• be able to use the school's library system to find out information;
• know how to find information in a book;
• use skimming and scanning techniques to locate information;
• be able to read a paragraph for the main idea and express it in one sentence;
• know how to make notes, order them and write from them;
• present information using different modelling procedures appropriately;
• be able to use a wide variety of resources to find information.

113

Minibeasts

Creepy-crawlies both fascinate and frighten children, but they all have opinions about them. They are fairly easy to catch and look after, which makes them a good topic to study.

Speaking and listening
The children can:
• discuss insects which they like;
• discuss insects which frighten them;
• talk about how they could set up an area in the school grounds for wildlife;
• listen to and learn songs about minibeasts.

Reading
• *The Very Hungry Caterpillar* and *The Bad-tempered Ladybird* by Eric Carle (Puffin).
• Stories by Beatrix Potter (Warne).
• Traditional stories about minibeasts, such as the legend of Arachne and the Caribbean stories about Anansi the spider-man.
• *Charlotte's Web* by E. B. White (Puffin).
• *Spiders* by T. Jennings and D. Anstey ('Into Science' series, Oxford University Press).

• 'Crickets' by Valerie Worth, 'Chameleon' by Alan Brownjohn and 'Rhymes for a bluebottle' by Libby Houston, all from *Marbles in my pocket*, chosen by Moira Andrew (Macmillan).
• 'Clockface' by Judith Thurman, from *A Fourth Poetry Book*, chosen by John Foster (Oxford University Press).
• 'Snails' by Tony Charles, 'Insects' by J Walsh and 'Dragonfly' by John Cotton, all from *Language in Colour*, chosen by Moira Andrew (Belair).
• 'Spider's Song' by Judith Nicholls, from her collection *Magic Mirror* (Faber & Faber).

Writing
The children can:
• brainstorm the word 'minibeast', writing as many words as possible in two minutes;

• look at a creature in a magnifying box and write in as much detail as possible about what they can see;
• invent some metaphors and similes about minibeasts;
• measure an area of a square metre in the grounds and map the creatures that they find there; then write a sentence about each one and use the sentences to create a poem;
• put a snail on a formica-topped desk, place a little

vegetation near it and make notes about how the snail moves and eats;
• use their observations of the snail to write stories about it;
• make a terrarium and record what happens to the rotting leaves sprinkled on top;
• lie flat in the grass and imagine what it would be like to be two centimetres tall;
• write and illustrate how a spider makes a web;
• draw the life cycle of a minibeast;
• make a diagram to categorise minibeasts by physical attributes or habitat.

Spelling
Ask the children to:
• make a letter string master for 'sn' words;
• make a word master for 'fly' words;
• make a word search for the names of minibeasts;
• make a list of minibeasts and put it in alphabetical order.

Handwriting
The children can:
• practise drawing undulating, even lines like a snail trail;
• practise diagonal joins with words like 'snail';
• practise horizontal lines with words like 'worm';
• write out and illustrate poems about minibeasts, their own or published ones.

Information skills
The children should, where appropriate:
• know the alphabet;
• use a dictionary, glossary or thesaurus to explore unusual or hard words;
• use the school's library confidently to research information;
• be able to find a useful book and use it for research;
• be able to make notes and write them up;
• know how to present information using a variety of modelling techniques;
• use a variety of resources to obtain detailed information on the topic.

Ourselves

This topic has meaning for children from a very young age. It can be used at different ages as part of a spiral curriculum, revisiting the topic to explore other aspects which build upon previous knowledge but require different skills and concepts.

Speaking and listening
The children can:
• discuss the stages of life, rites of passage and ceremonies;
• talk about how we need to care for our bodies, and the need for exercise, washing, clothing, health and nutrition;
• invite visitors such as a nurse or doctor, dentist, police officer or road safety officer to talk to them;

• discuss harmful agents such as smoking, drugs and alcohol, and also bullying, fighting, stealing, destroying and frightening others;
• discuss how we recognise each other;
• talk about caring for other people and their property;
• discuss how we make friends and how we destroy friendship and trust;
• discuss ways in which we can keep safe at home and outside;
• debate subjects like pocket money, bedtimes, making choices, independence;
• interview older people about their childhood and make comparisons;
• describe a member of the class without naming him, and let the others guess who it is.

Reading
• The *Alfie* books by Shirley Hughes (Fontana).
• *A Birthday for Frances* and *Bedtime for Frances* by Russell Hoban (Hippo).

• *My Naughty Little Sister* by Dorothy Edwards (Mammoth).
• *Hello Aurora* by A. C. Vestly (Puffin).
• *When I Was Little* by M. Walker (Puffin).
• *Topsy and Tim* books by Jean and Gareth Adamson (Blackie).
• *Not Now, Bernard* by David McKee (Andersen Press).
• *Cat on the Mat* by Brian Wildsmith (Oxford University Press).
• *Carrie's War* by Nina Bawden (Puffin).
• *Tom's Midnight Garden* by Philippa Pearce (Puffin).
• *Elidor* by Alan Garner (Fontana).
• *How your body works* (Usborne).
• *Little Body Books* (Macdonald).
• Poems from *Another First Poetry Book* and *A Fourth Poetry Book*, both chosen by John Foster (Oxford University Press).
• Poems from *Marbles in my pocket* (Macdonald) and *The unicorn and lions* (Belair), both chosen by Moira Andrew.

Writing

Ask the children to:
• brainstorm words to do with ourselves;
• write about a family outing at which everything seemed to go wrong;
• plan a birthday party, writing a guest list, invitations, lists of food and drink, instructions for party games, recipes for party food, etc;
• draw a cartoon story about the day my tooth fell out;
• write a poem called 'My hands can...';
• make charts to show their eye colour, hair colour, height, etc;
• write a story about a visit to the dentist, doctor or hospital;
• write about their earliest memories;
• keep a diary for a week;
• address an envelope to school, and one to themselves;
• draw their family tree;
• write five phrases to describe themselves, without using their names, so that others can guess who is described.

Spelling

The children can:
• draw themselves and label the drawing as fully as possible;
• make a list of 'person' words and put it in alphabetical order;
• look for the words within the words 'father' and 'mother keeping letter continuity and order'.

Handwriting

The children can :
• practise joining 'o' to other letters;
• write street names on a map;
• write the names of the members of their family;
• write labels for a display on the topic 'Ourselves'.

Information skills

The children should, where appropriate:
• know the alphabet;
• know how to use the school's library to research information;
• be able to find a useful book and use it for research;
• be able to make notes and write them up;
• know how to present information using a variety of modelling techniques;
• be able to use a variety of resources to obtain detailed information on the topic.

Paper

Paper is used daily in a variety of forms by everyone, in and out of school. It can be written on, painted, shaped, sculpted, printed on, torn and moulded.

Speaking and listening
The children can:
• talk about the different uses for paper at home and at school;
• talk about the use of wood and water in paper making;
• talk about the effect of printing presses upon communication;
• discuss the advantages of recycling paper in terms of the greenhouse effect, saving energy, saving on imports, decreasing the need for land-fill sites, and so on.

Reading
• *The Jolly Postman* by Janet and Alan Ahlberg (Heinemann).
• *The Paper-bag Princess* by Robert N. Munsch (Hippo).
• *Alice's Adventures in Wonderland* by Lewis Carroll.
• *The Father Christmas Letters* by J. R. R. Tolkien (Unwin Hyman).
• *The Stone Book* by Alan Garner (Collins).
• 'Posting Letters' by Gregory Harrison and 'This Letter's to Say' by Raymond Wilson, both from *A Fourth Poetry Book*, chosen by John Foster (Oxford University Press).
• 'Happy Birthday, Dilroy' by John Agard, from his collection *I Din Do Nuttin* (Magnet).
• 'Barn Owl' by Roger Elkin, from *The unicorn and lions*, chosen by Moira Andrew (Belair).
• 'Paper Boat' by Gerda Mayer and 'Delicious' by Leonard Clark, from *The first lick of the lolly* by Moira Andrew (Belair).
• 'If All the World were Paper' (traditional).
• Ask the children to research the ways of recording information before paper was invented, and to find out about the paper-making process.
• The children can investigate origami, its origins and uses.

Writing
Ask the children to:
• write a story about what the world would be like 'If all the world were paper...';
• list paper products and state the type of paper needed for each;
• write some instructions for making paper by hand and compare them with the process of manufacturing paper;
• make a chart to show how paper is used in industry, schools and the home;
• collect examples of paper products, make a collage and label it;

- design and make something in origami, and write instructions for someone to copy the design;
- design a packet for an Easter egg, draw the net and label it with folding instructions;
- make a flow chart of the processes involved in recycling paper;
- design a poster advertising a paper-collecting scheme for the school;
- make a time line to show the major developments in paper and printing;
- devise and record an experiment to test the strengths of different papers.

Spelling

The children can:
- use a letter string master for 'er' in words and the prefix 're';
- use a word master for 'new' words.

Handwriting

The children can:
- write out their own or published poems about paper;
- practise the letter 'p' and diagonal joins.

Information skills

The children should, where appropriate:
- know the alphabet;
- be able to use a dectionary, glossary and thesaurus to explore unusual or hard words;
- be able to use the school's library confidently to research information;
- be able to find a useful book and use it for research;
- be able to make notes and write them up;
- know how to present information using a variety of modelling techniques;
- be able to use a variety of resources to obtain detailed information on the topic.

Teddy bears

Teddy bears are popular with people of all ages the whole world over. They have been written about, sung about and owned by famous people, and can be worth thousands of pounds.

Speaking and listening
The children can:
• discuss teddy bears; who has one, where it sleeps; where it came from, how old it is, what it looks like and so on;
• discuss what it is about teddy bears that makes them so popular;
• listen to stories about teddy bears;
• make up words to describe a collection of bears, for example a 'hug' of bears.

Reading
• *Winnie the Pooh* by A. A. Milne (Methuen).

• *Teddy Robinson* by J. G. Robinson (Puffin).
• The *Teddy Bear* books by Susanna Gretz (A & C Black).
• The *Paddington* books by Michael Bond (Fontana).
• *Teddy's First Christmas* by A. Davidson (Fontana).
• *The Teddy Robber* by Ian Beck (Doubleday).
• *A Teddy Bear's Picnic*, stories chosen by T. Denton (Oxford University Press).
• *I Hate my Teddy Bear* by David McKee (Sparrow).

Writing
The children can:
• brainstorm teddy bear words;
• list the names of teddy bears;

• make a chart to show which children have teddy bears and how many they have;
• write a poem with the chorus line 'I love my teddy bear';
• write a letter requesting information about the Teddy Bears' Club, *Hugglets,* the teddy bear magazine or the Wareham Teddies Shop;
• research and write about how teddy bears came into being;

- find out and write about the oldest, the smallest, the largest bear and the fastest bears;
- write about the teddy bears of the famous;
- find out about Mishka (the 1980 Olympic symbol) and write an article about him;
- look for advertisements using teddy bears, and then devise one of their own;
- find out about teddy bear rallies and make a poster to advertise one;
- make up a name for a teddy bear and write a story about it;
- write a cartoon story for younger children about a teddy bear, with narrative as well as speech bubbles.

Spelling
The children can:
- look up any unknown words, list them and their meanings;
- use letter string masters for 'dy' in words;
- use a word master for 'ear' words;
- find or make up suitable teddy bear names for each letter of the alphabet.

Handwriting
Ask the children to:
- write descriptive labels for a teddy bear display;
- write out and illustrate a poem about a teddy bear;
- practise diagonal joins.

Information skills
The children should, where appropriate:
- know the alphabet;
- be able to put words in alphabetical order;
- know how to use a dictionary, glossary and thesaurus;
- be able to use the school's library system to find information;
- know how to find information in a book;
- be able to use skimming and scanning techniques to locate information;
- be able to read a paragraph and express the main idea in one sentence;
- know how to make, order and write up notes;
- present information using different modelling procedures;
- be able to use a wide variety of sources to find information.

Witches

Magical happenings have a great attraction for children, but be aware that some parents have an aversion to their children hearing about witches and the supernatural.

Speaking and listening
The children can:
• discuss what it would be like to have the power to change things;
• play a memory game – 'In my magic cauldron I put...';
• talk about the history of All Hallows' Eve;
• read out their favourite witch poems;
• dress up and role-play a fantasy character;
• role-play a chat-show interview with a witch;

• debate whether there are such things as good or bad witches;
• discuss the things that frighten them and why;
• create a play for Hallowe'en;
• discuss the pros and cons of 'trick or treat'.

Reading
• *Meg and Mog* by Helen Nicoll and Jan Pienkowski (Puffin).
• The *Worst Witch* books by Jill Murphy (Puffin).
• *Wobble the Witch Cat* by Mary Calhoun (World's Work).
• *The Witch of Monopoly Manor* by M. Stuart Barry (Fontana).
• *The Little Witch* by Margaret Mahy (A & C Black).
• *The Magic Finger* by Roald Dahl (Puffin).
• *Mary Poppins* by P. L. Travers (Puffin).
• *The Witch's Daughter* by Nina Bawden (Puffin).
• *The Ghost of Thomas Kempe* by Penelope Lively (Puffin).
• *Children of Green Knowe* by Lucy M. Boston (Puffin).

• Poems from *Go and open the door*, chosen by Moira Andrew (Macmillan Educational).
• 'The Hour when the Witches Fly' by John Foster, from his anthology *Another First Poetry Book* (Oxford University Press).
• 'Witch, Witch' by Ivy O. Eastwick and 'Gretchen in the Kitchen' by Jack Prelutsky, both from *Dragon Smoke*, chosen by Wes Magee (Basil Blackwell).
• Poems from *The Magic Tree*, chosen by David Woolger (Oxford University Press).
• Shakespeare's *Macbeth* (IV.i.4).

Writing
Ask the children to:
• draw a magical character and label it;
• brainstorm words on witches and magic, and write a poem using those words;
• make a collage of witches and give them names;
• make a wall picture with scenes from fairy tales, and write synopses of the different stories;
• create and collect phrases for spells;

Magic Cauldron

one, two wake up broom
three, four swept the floor

Eye of newt and hair of dog brings the rain and hail and fog.

Bubble Bubble Boil and Trouble

Boc of Spells

- draw a 'before and after' picture and create a spell for the transformation;
- make a magical puppet and write a play for it to perform;
- write a newspaper article about the sudden appearance of a number of black cats in a country village and the mysterious things that seem to have happened since their arrival;
- write a cartoon story for younger children about a witch whose spells always go wrong;
- collect phrases that explore feelings of suspense;
- write a poem with the starter line 'I feel frightened when...'.

Spelling
Ask the children to:
- list words from the brainstorming session in alphabetical order;
- create new words to describe witches and invent meanings for them;
- make a glossary of magic words;
- make a word search for 'itch' words;
- use a letter string master for 'ic' in words.

Handwriting
The children can:
- write out favourite poems for a personal anthology, and illustrate them;
- write out spells and display them coming out of a huge cauldron;
- practise the letter 'w' and horizontal joins.

Information skills
The children should, where appropriate:
- know the alphabet;
- be able to put words in alphabetical order;
- use a dictionary or thesaurus to explore unknown words;
- use contents lists, indexes, headings and tables to obtain information from books;
- be able to use skimming and scanning search techniques;
- present information in a variety of ways;
- use a variety of sources to investigate the topic.

CHAPTER 8

Assessment and record-keeping

Assessment provides information on what an individual pupil has experienced and on his or her level of achievement. Recording is the way in which the information is selected and stored.

Assessment gives feedback on a pupil's achievement and experience, and enables individual needs, strengths and weaknesses to be identified. However, assessment has to have an agreed purpose, and should be based on clear and relevant criteria from class schemes of work, school guidelines, National Curriculum documents and programmes of study. It should cover four elements:

- knowledge;
- concepts;
- skills;
- attitudes.

'Knowledge' is the information we acquire and our understanding of it. Through knowledge we develop concepts, skills and attitudes.

'Concepts' are the ideas through which we classify, organise and come to understand things we have learned. They are formed from generalising or abstracting information from a number of experiences.

'Skills' are the abilities we develop which enable us to perform tasks. They have to be refined through practice.

'Attitudes' are the ways we think and act in a variety of situations.

It is not the pupil that is assessed, but the evidence he provides about what he knows, understands and can do. The range of evidence needs to be wide and comprehensive, and weighted at different times on different aspects of the curriculum according to a child's stage of development.

Children need to be involved in identifying the evidence they will provide for assessment and reviewing. By reviewing their portfolio, they have proof of how much they know and the extent to which they have moved on.

The evidence can be collected through:
• observation;
• pupil/teacher interaction;
• written work;
• two- and three-dimensional work samples;
• portfolios;
• records of achievement;
• folders;
• files.

We use a variety of tools to assess pupils:
• published tests;
• teacher devised tests;
• diagnostic techniques;
• self-assessment;
• marking;
• pupil profiles;
• portfolios;
• video or tape recordings.

The recording method used should be constant throughout the school. It should be ongoing and formative, and helpful when planning work for the class or for a particular pupil. The records should enable teachers to set targets for their pupils, and to keep tabs on what the pupils have achieved or experienced. Photocopiable pages 175 to 185 give a selection of proformas to help with assessment and recording.

What is assessment?

Assessment is a necessary part of the process of matching activities to a child's developmental stage and establishing her readiness to move on. It is also needed to explore children's knowledge, conceptual development and attitudes to learning, in order to teach them to their best advantage.

There are several purposes for assessment.
• To provide a baseline for teaching.
We need to find out what children already know; that is, the hardest thing a child can do and the easiest thing she cannot. We also need to find out what children need to know; and how they can be helped to acquire particular skills, knowledge or concepts.

Published tests? Teacher devised tests? Self-assessment? Pupil profiles? Diagnostic techniques? Marking? Portfolios? Video or tape recording?

• To help identify particular learning needs, strengths and weaknesses.
By doing this, we can build on the child's strengths and use them to strengthen weaknesses.
• To find out a pupil's ability to cope with work.
This helps us to know whether the work given is within his or her range of competence and confidence.
• To identify errors that have been made, and find the reasons for them.
We can then analyse gaps in learning or specific areas of weakness.
• To monitor standards enabling us to examine both practice and continuity.
• To find out how much a pupil has gained, and therefore judge the effectiveness of the teaching.
• To ensure continuity across the curriculum and between classes enabling us to build on previous learning.
• To give children feedback on their learning, to show them the effectiveness of their learning strategies.

We get to know children's ability by:
• talking with them;
• observing how they perform a task;
• testing them against specific criteria;
• examining records of their work;
• discussing their work with others.

Before deciding which testing procedure to adopt, decisions have to be made about what we need to know of a child's performance on a learning task. Do we want to test what he has learned or how he has learned it? Do we want to analyse his knowledge of a subject, his skills, the concepts he has acquired, or his attitudes?

We also have to decide:
• what needs to be assessed;
• how best to assess those areas;
• how we are going to record the results;
• the use we shall make of the records.

Different ages of children require different forms of assessment.

Teachers of nursery and reception classes will need to consider how they can effectively assess the progress of the very young. If from observation, how and when will they observe? If using criterion referenced assessment (see page 130), how will it be constructed?

How far do teachers need to go at the upper end of the primary stage? How will the different methods come together to form a continuous pattern of assessment?

When developing a whole-school policy, these are some of the questions to be addressed.

Devising an assessment policy

Each school's policy documents will change and develop in line with new knowledge and understanding of how children learn, and taking into account declared Government policies, profile components, attainment targets or assessment tests. Each school has to consider what the implications of all these things are for its own schemes of work.

One way of doing this is to ask questions.
• Where are we now?
• How do our guidelines and schemes of work compare with new knowledge or Government policy documents?

• What would we ideally like our children to be able to do?
• How are we going to achieve that?

This process works well for all curriculum areas, but let's look at how one school examined its English policy documents.

Firstly, in this school, the teachers took a critical look at work throughout the school and checked for coverage and continuity. They collected work done by pupils during the earlier part of the year and checked to see how close it was to the National Curriculum requirements. They also began to monitor children closely. Each teacher chose three children of varying levels of ability, observing them over a period of two weeks, keeping copies of their work and a diary of their activities and progress. They then brought the work samples to a staff meeting and placed them under the appropriate headings for Levels 1 to 6.

Pairs of teachers then took a pile and argued the case for each piece of work being in that level.

The breadth of ability in any one level was much more obvious when the work of children just moving into one level and others just moving on to the next was seen side by side.

The school took from the Government policy documents headings for general provision and detailed provision, drawing out information in the form of a checklist to compare with their own policy documents.

The ideal standard for each child was considered with caution, bearing in mind the difficulties of resourcing, staffing and buildings, but trying not to let these things become excuses. In the meantime the records kept by each teacher were examined. Although they covered similar ground, none was strikingly the best.

The teachers decided to start again with a standard format for recording each child's progress. It had to be simple, clear, quick to fill in, useful to the next teacher and meaningful for the pupil (where appropriate), the parents and the governors. This record sheet was to be used for a term and then revised in the light of usage.

The record sheet has to reveal gaps as well as showing movement through the attainment targets in English, while recognising that a hierarchical ladder was not appropriate in English. The teachers looked at the most useful way of recording information and chose to use ticks, circles and different coloured pencils for each year. They discussed the benefit to the child of colouring in her own block on completion, and it was thought that this would help the child to have a sense of her own progress – if handled properly. They reminded themselves that most children take two years, some even more, to go through each Level and that while they needed to stretch their children, they should do so with the smallest of steps, building on previous learning.

But what kind of assessment would indicate when a child had completed a level? These are some of the measures that they discussed.
• Observation of the time spent on a task, the child's attitude to English, what he could do for himself, and where he sought help.
• Tape recordings of speech one-to-one, in small groups, and in class discussion, concentrating on only three or four children over a period of time.
• Testing – standardised tests set by LEA or Government, and school-based ones to identify gaps.
• Conferencing – individually by the teacher, or by the peer group with the aid of a tape-recorder.
• Marking with the child present and recording the development evident in the writing or the ensuing discussion.

• Using individual reading records or reading logs.
• Using the school's revised checklist for each of the language modes to ensure that the English curriculum had sufficient breadth and depth.
• The teachers discussed the question of how it would be possible to assess children in classes of around 30. What would happen to the rest of the class if the teacher was closeted with one child? They concluded that it couldn't be done like that. Any assessment and testing to be done would have to be possible within the normal classroom.

They realised that there was no need for anxiety about assessment. Teachers have always been assessing children, because it provides

the information needed to structure future teaching and learning, as well as ensuring breadth and continuity across the curriculum areas and between classes. Assessment has been and must continue to be the servant, not the master of the curriculum.

Types of assessment

There are several main types of assessment, each serving a different purpose.
• Assessment of readiness, to find out whether a child has the skills needed to commence a programme of work or a learning task.
• Assessment before placement, to identify what a child's abilities and attitudes are and how he will fit into a particular class (especially for new entrants).

• Formative assessment, to monitor on a continual basis a child's progress through a programme, to provide reinforcement, to find gaps in learning and to identify faulty learning styles.
• Diagnostic assessment, to identify errors and learning problems; specially designed for a task to determine persistent difficulties.
• Summative assessment, to judge, at the conclusion of programme or task, the finished product, level reached and degree of mastery of objectives; to analyse teaching of objectives and the efficiency and suitability of teaching styles, to find out the best a child can do; to assess his normal response.
• Norm referenced assessment, to ascribe standardised ranking in a given population, the school, local area, county or country, by means of formal testing.
• Criterion referenced assessment, to assess a child's ability over a given number of tasks; the knowledge she has in a particular subject area; and her progress or mastery over specific skills.

Types of records

Whatever records are kept, they must:
• have a clear purpose;
• be easy to complete;
• provide information for future planning;
• provide the basis for discussions about progress between child, teacher and parent;
• be of a manageable size.
    All information should be dated and bear the name and status of the record-keeper.
    The following are some examples of different sorts of records and their contents.

Teaching plan
This should include details of:
• what you are going to teach;
• how you are going to teach it;
• the learning opportunities;
• the group size;
• the resources needed;
• how the finished work will be presented.

Checklist
This should record what children have achieved in concepts, knowledge and skills across the curriculum.

Observation
Observational records should provide an account of what is actually seen, not the teacher's thoughts or feelings.

Personal profiles

These should provide significant information about pupils, covering the complete curriculum range, and indicating both process and product, including:
• evidence of knowledge, concepts and skills acquired;
• attitude towards curriculum areas;
• relationships with peers and with adults;
• the topics covered and the pupil's response;
• the pupil's self-evaluations, completed at regular intervals.

Portfolios

These are files or folders of work containing:
• a range of written work;
• visual material in the form of pictures, diagrams and charts, layouts and photographs;
• tapes of oral work.

Pupils' handmade books

• Topic or personal project books;
• selected writing collected over a period of time;
• stories for peers or younger children.

Parent/teacher communication

Notes from meetings with parents, and letters from them.

Records for specific purposes

These could include:
• collated information for pupils transferring to other schools;
• records of attendance and related information;
• any involvement with outside agencies such as school psychological service, social services, medical agencies;
• any testing and provision for special needs.

English attainment targets and statements of attainment

The following four pages each show a matrix to illustrate an aspect or aspects of English; speaking and listening, reading, writing, and spelling and handwriting.

Each matrix is divided into four areas of achievement, each with six levels, which indicate broad bands of development – Beginning; Making a start; Moving forward; Competent; Able; Exceptionally able. These bands of development correspond to Levels 1 to 6 within the National Curriculum.

The matrices can be used to identify which level a child has reached in each area of each aspect of English, to indicate which level the pupil should work towards, to plan the English curriculum for the class or to draw out areas that can be covered in cross-curricular topic work.

Speaking and listening

Assessment should be informal, incidental and continuous. Listening and speaking are reciprocal, each dependent on the other. Clarity and plain speaking affects the quality of listening.

	Give an account	Performance	Discussion and collaboration	Information and explanation
Beginning	Speak clearly and express needs. Listen when others speak.	Respond to stories and poems.	Participate as a speaker and listener in group activities.	Make relevant responses to simple instructions.
Making a start	Describe events, real or imagined, to the teacher or another pupil.	Participate as a speaker in a group. Talk about poems and stories heard or read.	Participate in discussion on a given task within a group.	Listen to stories and ask relevant questions. Make relevant responses to a range of more complex instructions and give simple instructions in turn.
Moving forward	Relate an event in connected narrative to the class, group or a known adult.	Relate events to interested others. Ask questions and comment on what has been said.	Listen, comment, question and respond to what is said by other children and adults.	Convey accurately a simple message. Give, receive and follow accurately precise instructions for a task as an individual or within a group.
Competent	Give an accurate, detailed account of an event, something learned or why a course of action was taken.	Take part in group presentation.	Participate as listener and speaker in a group discussion on issues. Express a personal view and comment constructively on what is being discussed or experienced.	Ask and respond to a whole range of questions with growing confidence.
Able	Give a well-organised, sustained account of an event, personal experience or activity.	Participate in a group presentation, and contribute to the planning.	Contribute constructively to a discussion or debate, developing ideas and advocating or justifying a point of view.	Use appropriate language to convey information and explain ideas effectively in straightforward situations.
Exceptionally able	Contribute to group discussion, responding sensitively to the opinions of others.	Help to plan, organise and take part in a group presentation or performance with some fluency and confidence.	Contribute well-considered opinions to group discussions. Offer statements of personal feelings in response to the contributions of others.	Use appropriate language to convey information and ideas in a variety of situations on a subject familiar to the audience or other participants.

Reading

The teacher should assess reading through structured observation. Assessment should be continuous and cover a range of different materials and contexts.

	Range and fluency	Response	Study Skills	Knowledge about language
Beginning	Show signs of a developing interest in reading.	Talk about stories, recalling important incidents. Talk about information from non-fiction texts.	Show some recognition of single words or letters in familiar context.	Recognise that print, wherever found, carries meaning.

Making a start	Read and understand simple labels, signs and notices. Read a range of print with some independence, fluency, accuracy and understanding.	Recall what has happened thus far in a story and predict possible outcomes.
		  Express opinions informed by information from a range of reading material.
			Show alphabet knowledge through use of word books and simple dictionaries.
			  Use a variety of cues in reading – picture, context, sight and phonic.
				Understand that simple sentences obey rules of word order.

Moving forward	Read familiar stories and poems with fluency and expression. Read silently with sustained concentration.	Listening attentively to stories and talk about the plot, characters and setting, recalling significant details. In responding to stories and poetry, indicate the beginnings of inference, deduction and going beyond the literal meaning. Give evidence, in writing and discussion, of beginning to understand story structure.	Devise questions to help in selecting appropriate reference and information sources from a library.	Recognise that words which sound the same can have different meanings.
Competent	Read aloud, from a range of familiar literature, with fluency and expresssion.	Reading from a wide range of literature and give reasons for preferences. Respond to fiction showing a developing use of inference, deduction and previous reading experience, and recognising authorial clues to story outcomes.	Use catalogue, classification or information retrieval system to locate books and media sources when seeking facts or other data.	Recognise that words can have more than one meaning.
Able	Show an ability to explain preferences clearly, after reading from a wide range of poetry and fiction.	Respond to literature and non-fiction, supporting own views by using details from the text. In discussion, show signs of recognising whether non-literary and media texts are fact or opinion.	Use retrieval systems and organisational devices to find answers to queries.	Recognise word play, puns and jokes, and discuss the effect of the choice of words upon the reader's response.
Exceptionally able	Use references to the text to illustrate preferences over a wide range of children's literature and older fiction.	Respond to literature and non-fiction, making judgements and supporting opinions from the text, as appropriate. Identify some ways in which distinction can be made between fact and opinion.	Identify key points on particular issues from a range of materials using own information-retrieval skills	Discuss changes in word meanings and usage over distance and time, supported from reading or personal experience.

Writing

Assessment should be based on a range of writing activities. Samples of writing should be kept in the pupil's portfolio so that the range of writing and its development is evident and can be monitored.

	Structure and organisation	Variety and audience	Style	Revising and redrafting
Beginning	Recognise that using pictures, symbols, letters, words or phrases communicates meaning.	Communicate meaning using pictures, symbols, letters, words or phrases.	Structure communication left to right in sequential order.	Add symbols, letters, words and phrases to pictures to communicate ideas.
Making a start	Write, independently, in complete sentences. Some boundaries indicated by capital letters and full stops.	Produce simple, clear and coherent chronological and non-chronological writing.	Structure chronological events sequentially, whether real or imagined.	Read through work after completion adding letters, words or punctuation in discussion with the teacher.
Moving forward	Produce, independently, written work showing use of complete sentences, mainly using capital letters and full stops correctly.	Produce a range of fiction and non-fiction writing for different purposes.	Produce a range of fiction and non-fiction writing with a defined beginning, middle and end. Use a wider range of connectives than 'and' and 'then'.	Begin to revise and redraft, in discussion with adults or peers, checking for clarity of meaning, suitability to purpose, and surface features such as correct and consistent use of tenses and pronouns.
Competent	Produce written work showing a growing ability to structure simple subject matter, making it clear to the reader by using sentence punctuation correctly and beginning to punctuate direct speech.	Produce a range of fiction and non-fiction writing which has a defined opening, setting, series of events and resolution.	Order non-chronological writing in a variety of ways according to its purpose.	Redraft and revise own writing independently and discuss reasons for changes made.
Able	Structure writing by using correct layout for both fiction and non-fiction, eg headings and paragraphing. Use correct sentence and dialogue punctuation, with simple use of commas.	Write, to engage the reader, in a variety of forms for a range of different purposes.	Write in Standard English, except where the purpose requires non-standard forms, showing knowledge of the differentiation between speech and writing.	Make notes, and assemble and order notes and ideas on paper, on VDU, or in discussion with others. Produce an initial draft and revise as necessary.
Exceptionally able	Produce written work which is well organised and clearly set out using sentences and dialogue punctuation correctly, a wide use of commas and beginning to use brackets and pairs of dashes.	Present subject matter appropriately for specified but known audiences.	Use stylistic features, and those which characterise an impersonal style, using Standard English except in contexts which demand non-standard forms.	Recognise times when planning, drafting, redrafting and revising are appropriate, and carry out such processes on paper or VDU.

Spelling and handwriting

Spelling and handwriting are combined in this table. The first three sections relate to spelling, and the last one to handwriting and presentation.

	Correct spelling	Word patterns	Knowledge of language	Handwriting and presentation
Beginning	Begin to write letter shapes in response to speech sounds and letter names.	Represent whole words by single letters or groups of letters.	Understand the difference between drawing and writing.	Show some control over word size, shape and orientation of writing.　Use drawing to present ideas and stories.
Making a start	Spell some common words, but not necessarily correctly.	Know that spelling has patterns, and use that knowledge to deduce spellings of a wider range of words.	Know the names of letters and their order in the alphabet.	Use upper and lower case consistently, correctly and legibly.　Use artwork to present written work, eg cards, messages, stories.
Moving forward	In own writing, spell simple polysyllabic words of common patterns correctly.	Use correctly the knowledge of regular vowel patterns and letter strings.	Evidence an awareness of the relationships of word families.	Start to develop a clear joined writing style.　Use word processor and artwork to present final copy.
Competent	In own writing, spell main word patterns, including common prefixes and suffixes, correctly.	In own writing, spell correctly words which contain the main patterns in English.	Begin to correct own spellings when redrafting.	In independent work, use clear, fluent joined writing style.　Begin to use presentational devices, eg artwork, handwriting, typewriter and computer printout.
Able	In own writing, spell correctly words of increasing complexity, including inflectional suffixes which require consonant doubling or -e deletions.	In own writing, spell correctly words of increasing complexity.	Correct own spellings when redrafting copy, using dictionaries or other word stores.	Write clearly and legibly in both printed and cursive style.　Use a range of lettering styles for headings and a variety of presentational devices for body of copy.
Exceptionally able	Use related word patterns to assist spelling, eg stressed and unstressed syllables as in pirate/piratical.	Recognise that words with related meanings, while sounding different, often have related spellings, eg lyric/lyricist, sign/signature.	Use dictionary, computer spell-check facility and other word stores to check spellings when redrafting copy.	Write fluently and legibly. Use presentational devices appropriate to the task, including computer graphics and desk-top publishing. Finished work well laid out and presented clearly and attractively.

Observation

When using observation to collect evidence, we need to have clear criteria for what is to be observed. We need to focus on particular issues that will be useful and record things which are significant and relevant.

When selecting what you wish to observe, it is better to take two or three items and cover them well with a few children at a time. This way the observation slips easily into the school day and is less likely to become a chore.

Make a chart of the pupils' names and head the columns with the items you wish to observe. Place it in a file on your desk, and keep a pencil with it. As you receive evidence that a child has mastered an item – from talking with her, watching her or marking her work with her – it is easy to tick your sheet. An additional column allows for any comment you may wish to make.

Speaking and writing, the output processes, are relatively easy to check over time, but the input modes of language, the 'silent activities' of listening and reading, are more difficult.

When listening, we tend to link what we hear to prior knowledge or past experience and the mind slides into other realms. But this doesn't mean that our listening skills are deficient.

As adults we rarely read aloud and, if asked to do so, may feel vulnerable and threatened. Maybe this stems from having to read aloud in class from texts at the limit of our reading competence, always conscious of the need for accuracy rather than following the meaning. This anxiety produces the mistakes we try so hard to avoid.

To check on input modes, teachers ask questions. But how do *we* feel when we are posed questions, or given points to discuss, after having listened to a talk presenting us with new ideas? How would we feel if we were asked searching questions by the librarian on returning a book?

School-wise children may well take to reading books below their reading competence, or avoid reading altogether, to avoid offering an incorrect answer.

If we are observing a child, rather than making inferences, we need to record factually what the child is doing over a period of time and in differing situations. We also need to devise a proforma which allows interpretations to be made of these facts.

Observations should be ongoing, made at odd moments during the day and analysed regularly, at least every half term. Other adults should contribute to the observation profile, especially parents.

All recording should state what a child *can* do; we will know from the omissions what areas need to be worked on.

Portfolios

It is impossible to maintain a complete portfolio of the range of work children produce, containing evidence of all the significant steps they have made throughout their primary years. However, the evidence kept should truly reflect the child's progress; it should also supply sufficient information and be of use in the future.

To prevent the portfolio becoming too unwieldy, questions have to be asked about what should be included. For example:
• Who or what is the evidence for?

• How can the range of work be reflected and how can significant steps be shown?
• To what extent can the children be involved in developing their own portfolios?

A full range of recent work should be included, but once a stage or level is passed, the collection should be reduced to that which is relevant in the long term. This way the portfolio or file is kept in manageable proportions. Photographs of displays, good work and presentations also record evidence without creating bulk.

Children need to be involved in selecting work for their portfolios because it reinforces what they know and shows them their progress. They find it fascinating to look back and see their own growth. This is considered more fully in the section on self-assessment (see page 142).

Informal reading inventories

Informal reading inventories (IRIs) are close observations of children's reading performance without recourse to formal, standardised tests. Material used should be at, or very close to, a child's instructional level if they are to be of real value in guiding or planning a programme for that pupil.

An IRI has a number of advantages over more formal procedures in that:
• it assesses the child's ability

in comparison with his own previous performance, not that of others;
• it is chosen by the teacher from familiar but not necessarily know material;
• it is appropriate to the child's own needs;
• it can be prepared from any type of reading material.

There are three main forms of IRIs:
• miscue analysis;
• running records;
• cloze procedure.

A brief outline of each of these methods follows. More detailed information can be found in some of the books referred to in the book list in Chapter 9.

The strength of informal reading inventories lies in the close match that can exist between what is tested and what is taught, between the needs the teacher has identified and the way he plans to provide for those perceived needs. The way the inventories are administered is not stressful to the pupil, and can therefore give a reasonably accurate picture of the stage the pupil has reached and the problems she has encountered in her reading.

Miscue analysis

Miscue analysis is a simple procedure from which you can determine:
• whether a book is at the right reading level for the reader;
• whether the book is at the right comprehension level;
• what the pattern of errors is and, therefore, how to develop appropriate teaching strategies.

The procedure for carrying out a miscue analysis is as follows:

• Select a passage of between 100 and 200 words, from a book of similar difficulty to the child's current reading. The selection should be capable of being read as a story.
• Write down the questions you want to ask, based on the information in the extract. Questions should help you to assess both the child's understanding of the factual content and her ability to draw conclusions from it.
• Make two copies of the sample text only, so that a picture or other writing does not provide additional clues to the reader. One copy is for the child, and the other for you to record on.
• Ask the child to read the passage, while you mark your copy using the code opposite. Tape record the reading so you can pick up later on any errors you may miss.
• Ask the child to read the passage again, silently. After removing the passage, ask the comprehension questions, and record the answers.
• Calculate the number of correct words as a percentage. Do the same with the comprehension answers.
• Examine the pattern of reading errors or difficulties and use this information to plan your future teaching strategies.

Recording the reading errors

Use a standardised code for analysis so that it can be interpreted by others.

- No response – cross through the word and tell the child, writing T above the word.
- Substitutions – underline the word and write the substituted word above it.
- Repetitions – underline the word or phrase repeated and write R above it.
- Omissions – circle the word or phrase left out.
- Insertions – use the insertion symbol and write the added word above.
- Reversals – underline the word and use a double-headed arrow.
- Mispronunciation – enclose the word in brackets ( ) and write MP above.
- Self-correction – write SC above the word which the child corrected unaided.
- Hesitation – write // where the delay occurred.
- Ignored punctuation – circle the missed punctuation.

The ~~lion~~ went on the bridge. (T)

The lion <u>went</u> on the bridge. (ran)

The lion went on <u>the</u> bridge. (R)

The lion (went) on the bridge.

The lion went on ^ the bridge. (to)

The lion went <u>on</u> the bridge.

The lion (went) on the bridge. (MP)

The lion went on the bridge. (no/sc)

The lion went on the // bridge.

The lion went on the bridge◯ He

Scoring

By working out percentages you can establish the level at which the child is coping with the material in terms of word accuracy and comprehension.

Method of calculation

Word accuracy:
Number of words in the passage = A

Number of errors = B

$$\frac{A-B}{A} \times 100 = \% \text{ word accuracy}$$

Comprehension:
Number of correct responses = C
Number of questions asked = D

$$\frac{C}{D} \times 100 = \% \text{ comprehension.}$$

When a child's word accuracy and comprehension percentages have been worked out, he or she can be assigned to one of three levels:

- Independent level – word accuracy of 95 per cent or above and comprehension of 90 per cent or above. These children can read fluently and extract information without much help.
- Instructional level – word accuracy of 90-94 per cent and comprehension of 75-90 per cent. These children will need some teaching support either before or during the reading.
- Frustration level – word accuracy below 90 per cent and comprehension below 75 per cent. These children have been struggling with material that is far too difficult. They will ignore punctuation and seek help rather than attempting to correct themselves.

Running records

Running records are a reliable way of finding out how well a child can read his present material, and provide information for planning his day-to-day learning.

The use of running records has come from the work of Marie Clay and is detailed in her book, *The Early Detection of Reading Difficulties* (Heinemann Educational, 1981).

Use running records to look at the child in relation to the texts level of difficulty – should she move on to harder material or back to easier texts? Use the records for grouping children or for finding the level of a new entrant to the class.

Work from a book the child has read only once or twice before. Use either a caption book or a complete passage from a story of between 100 and 200 words. Tape recording the reading helps the assessment to be more exact. Head a sheet of paper with the child's name, date of birth and the book title. Record each line of text using the key shown below and rule a line across the end of each page once it has been read.

Scoring
• Every correct or corrected word is credited.
• A number of attempts at a word, with eventual self-correction, is counted as a credit.
• Omissions, insertions and nil responses are counted as errors.
• Repeated errors are counted each time they are made.
• If a phrase is read wrongly, each word is counted as an error, but if each is subsequently corrected, then every one is counted as a self-correction.
• If a child makes nonsense of a line or page, ask him to 'try again'. This counts as one error rather than one for each confusion.

Method of calculation
Words in passage = A
Errors = B
Self-correction = C

$$\frac{A - B}{A} \times 100 = \text{\% word accuracy}$$

$$A \div B = \text{error rate}$$

$$\frac{B + C}{C} = \text{ratio of errors to self-corrections}$$

Correct reading: give a tick for each correct word	Come on Mum. ✓✓✓ Wake up.　　✓✓
Omissions	$\dfrac{-}{\text{Mum}}$ (word omitted)
Substitutions	$\dfrac{\text{Get}}{\text{Wake}}$ (substituted word) (correct word)
Self-correction	$\dfrac{\text{Get}}{\text{Wake}}$ | Sc (self-corrected on second attempt)
Repetitions	✓✓ R (Repeated two words)
Insertions	$\dfrac{\text{now}}{-}$ (Insertion)
No response	$\dfrac{-}{\text{Wake}}$ (No response)
Try that again	$\dfrac{-}{\text{Wake}}$ | $\dfrac{-}{\text{TTA}}$ | $\dfrac{\text{Sc}}{\text{T}}$ (Correct attempt) (No attempt, child told word)

Cloze procedure

Human beings have a tendency to make complete that which they consider is not complete. Cloze procedure is based upon this premise.

Words are deleted in a selected passage according to a chosen criteria. The purpose is for the child to close the gaps with what she considers an appropriate word.

This procedure assesses a child's reading and comprehension skills, as well as the match between her reading level and the book used. It can be used in direct teaching to improve reading strategies.

Cloze procedure requires the child to read the passage both forward and back to elicit the meaning. The passage has to be looked at as a complete entity in order to assess its meaning and syntactic structure, and each insertion has to be examined critically for its appropriateness to the passage.

The procedure is as follows:
• Select three passages, of between 150 and 200 words each, which form a complete passage either from one book or from books of the same readability level.
• Delete words either at random or according to their function. Random words can be every tenth, seventh or fifth word; every tenth word is the best way to start. Every seventh is common practice but can be quite difficult; every fifth is hard. Alternatively, you may choose to delete all the nouns, verbs, adjectives, pronouns or tenses. Do not delete words in the first or last sentences.
• Use one straight line to replace each deleted word, to allow for invented spelling. If you indicate the number of letters, a child may reject a word on the grounds that it 'doesn't fit', whereas the word may be correct but the problem is in the spelling of the word.
• You can set up a multiple choice, using a four- or five-word sample for children to select from. For example:

Katie climbed the apple
  bush
  hill
  see
  tree

• If a child is having problems with specific parts of a word, use cloze to focus attention on the difficulty. For example:
Katie ____ed the apple tree.
Katie cl ____ the apple tree.
• To enable your sheets to be used again, number the deletions so that the children

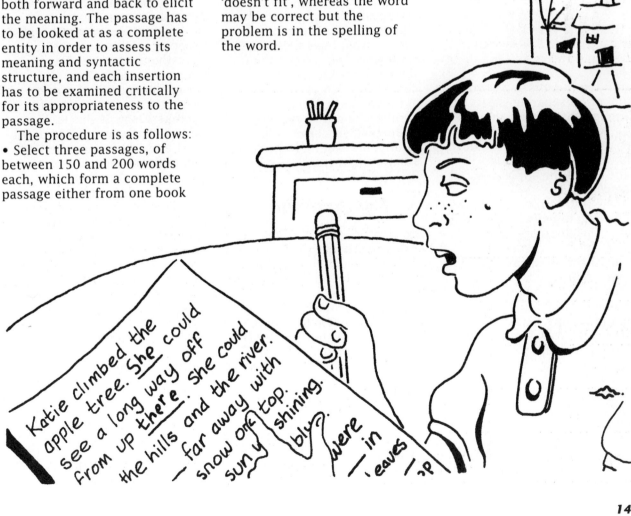

can fill in the missing words by number on separate sheets. It is important to place the number at the end of the gap, not the beginning, so as not to disrupt the reading flow.

Katie ____4 the apple tree.

Guidelines

It is helpful to remember the following guidelines when using the cloze procedure.

• Use the cloze procedure orally if the child's reading age is less than seven.

• Teach children how to do cloze by working orally first, then in groups.

• Try cloze with familiar texts before you use it for testing.

• Discuss as a group what words might be suitable to fill the gaps.

• The way you use cloze will depend on your purpose. If you are concerned with the child's reading rate, you will need to time the test. If your concern is for accuracy, you will consider the semantic responses. If you are concerned with creative imagination, you will look at the originality of the response.

• By using three passages from a particular book you can assess, from the child's responses, the suitability of the book's reading and comprehension level.

Cloze can be fun for children, and it engenders feelings of success rather than failure, motivating rather than frustrating them.

Self-assessment

As children grow through the primary school, they need to be increasingly involved in assessing their own work. In developing clear ideas about what makes a piece of work good, they begin to take more pride in what they do and how they do it. They also learn to be constructively critical, so increasing their inter-personal skills.

Reception children are well aware when they have completed a good piece of work. Ask them to put it in their good work folder. Every so often, go through the folder with them so they are involved in the decision of what to keep and what to take home. Be prepared, sometimes to bargain for the best piece. Let the child take it home to show the family, but ask him to bring it back and put it in his folder. Try to keep pieces which indicate progression. Don't forget to date each piece of work!

Children in the middle primary years should be involved in selecting work to keep in the same way, but with deeper discussion and more specific comments being made. Say why you want a piece of work put in their file and invite their reasons for pieces they want to include. From the age of six, children should start filling in the Reading Checklist (photocopiable page 183), together with the teacher, twice a year.

At the upper end of the junior school pupils can fill in self-assessment sheets, like those on photocopiable pages 181 and 182, during the first half of each term. Discuss each completed sheet with its author and plan for these declared needs.

At transfer to secondary school, a child's file will show clear evidence of the pace of his or her growth and progress throughout the primary years.

Topics and assessment

Topics are an ideal way to assess both oral and written language development because children work in a way that displays a range of knowledge, skills, concepts and achievements. These can be assessed by the teacher through observation; conferencing; set tasks or criteria; marking; presentation and display.

Children are more likely to show what they can really do if they are involved in activities which are familiar and normal for them, and have a clearly defined purpose. Through careful planning, assessment can be built into the topic programme, forming a natural part of class work rather than remaining a thing apart, different and unsettling.

List the areas in your planned scheme of work that you need to cover, revisit or reinforce in your topic. Enter them on a copy of the proforma on photocopiable page 175. This profile builds up to show the child's learning development through the primary years.

Marking

When the children have finished a piece of work, ask them to go through it using a check list similar to those on photocopiable pages 176 to 178, but adapted to suit the pupils in your class at their levels of ability. They should do this before they bring the work to you for marking.

Have an 'in' tray and, beside it, a list on which children can enter their names. That way you have a record of who has completed their assignment, and the first to finish is the first to be seen.

Mark in pencil. Children can become very negative about their work when it is returned to them stitched up with red embroidery.

Any comments, written or verbal, must begin by saying what is good about the child's work, and what you like about

it. Be specific. There is always something you can say – for example 'I did enjoy your story, especially the part where ...', or 'The dog was a real bundle of trouble, wasn't he?'

Use constructive comments, rather than negative criticism, about the things that you think could be changed to improve the work – for example, 'Have you thought of ....?' What if you ...?', 'How about trying ...?'

The most important thing is to remember that it is the child's work, not yours. It should say what she wants it to say, in the way she wants to say it. You can suggest changes, but don't make it your work. It is hers; let her keep ownership of it.

Assessment of the learning space

The organisation of your classroom and the way you work reflects your thoughts about education. Consider the following questions in relation to your working environment.
• What does your classroom look like? Does it reflect the school ethos? What aspects of it do you want to change? What prevents the changes taking place?

• What are your priorities? How do you cater for first-hand experiences? How do you organise resources? Are there opportunities for stimulation, reflection, privacy and silence? Is your classroom a language-rich one? How do you cater for reading, writing, research and drama?
• How much furniture was inherited from the previous incumbent? Is it needed? Is it the right height for your pupils? How is it arranged? Why? Is it easy to get away from your desk or are you hemmed in? Do you need a desk? Why? Is there a work-space equipped for mounting work and making books?
• Can you work alongside children? Do you read, write, paint and make things with them?
• How often do you use the blackboard? What do you write on it, and why?
• What do your children do when a visitor comes in to talk to you?

Your classroom is where you spend your working day. Make it one which is user-friendly, stimulating and where good teaching can take place.

CHAPTER 9

Books and resources

This chapter lists a wide range of books which can provide useful and interesting background reading to support your work in all areas of the English curriculum. Full bibliographic details have been given, and a short description of each book has been included to help you select the books you need.

A separate section deals with useful resources other than books, and the chapter ends with a list of suppliers and organisations connected with English teaching.

◄Reading corner

Books

Speaking and listening

Brown, Richard (1989) *The Spoken Word Project* (Oliver & Boyd). Contains useful ideas for developing and extending talk in the classroom.

Crystal, David *Listen to Your Child: A Parent's Guide to Children's Language* (Penguin). Valuable advice for parents (and teachers) on oral language development.

Norman, Kate (1990) *Teaching Talking and Learning in Key Stage One* (National Curriculum Council). This book, based on the work of the National Oracy Project, looks at children's talk and suggests ways in which talk can help them to learn.

Rosen, Betty (1988) *And None of It Was Nonsense* (Mary Glasgow Publications). An excellent book on the power of story-telling in school.

Reading

Applebee, Arthur (1978) *The Child's Concept of Story* (University of Chicago Press). A study of language use, concept development and responses to literature in children from two to seventeen.

Bettelheim, Bruno and Zelan, Karen (1978) *On Learning to Read: The Child's Fascination with Meaning* (Thames & Hudson). An assessment of the true value of reading, and a critical evaluation of the ways in which reading is taught.

Book Fax from the Children's Book Foundation. This is a mine of information on children's books and authors, and is continually being updated.

Butler, Dorothy (1986) *Five to Eight* (Bodley Head). Discusses ways of sharing books with five- to eight-year-olds, and recommends suitable books for children at each level.

Chambers, Aidan (1984) *Introducing Books to Children* (Heinemann Educational). Considers how active readers are made, and offers a critical blueprint for presenting and guiding discussions on books.

Children's Books of the Year. An annotated selection of the best recent children's books, published annually by the Andersen Press in association with Book Trust.

Cook, Elizabeth (1976) *The Ordinary and the Fabulous* (Cambridge University Press). An interpretation of myths and legends and the best ways of telling them.

Donaldson, Margaret (1984) *Children's Minds* (Fonatana). A fount of knowledge about how children learn.

Freeman, Sheila and Munns, Esther (1989) *Story Talk* (Macmillan Educational). Introduces children to a range

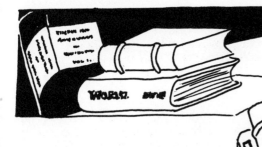

of contemporary fiction with practical suggestions for activities.

Heald, Chris and Eustace, Val (1988) *Ready to Read* (Hippo Books). A book designed for the parents of two- to six-year-old children, with practical ideas for reading activities.

Holdaway, Don (1979) *The Foundations of Literacy* (Ashton Scholastic) A useful book about the beginnings of literacy.

Liebe, Frankie (1985) *Bright Ideas: Reading Activities* (Scholastic Publications). Practical suggestions for reading activities and games.

Meek, Margaret (1986) *Learning to Read* (Bodley Head). A book to help parents understand what is happening when a child is taught to read. Useful for teachers, too!

Meek, Margaret, Warlow, Aidan and Barton, Griselda (1978) *The Cool Web* (Bodley Head). Essays discussing the experiences found in children's stories.

Moon, Cliff (ed) (1985) *Practical Ways to Teach Reading* (Ward Lock Educational). Examines the ways in which children learn to read, using a wide range of books and materials.

Moss, Elaine (1985) *Picture Books for Young People 9-13* (Thimble Press). A list of picture books examining various aspects of life.

Sommerfield, Muriel, Torbe, Mike and Ward, Colin (1983) *A Framework for Reading: Creating a Policy in the Primary School* (Heinemann). Discusses how to synthesise the varied experiences within a school's staff to create a reading policy.

Waterland, Liz (1988) *Read With Me: An Apprenticeship Approach to Reading* (Thimble Press). This book discusses how to make real readers, using real books.

Writing

Andrew, Moira (1989) *Language in Colour* (Belair Publications). An excellent book, which suggests various ways of using poetry as a starting point for environmental themes.

Bennet, Jill and Chambers, Aidan (1984) *Poetry for Children: A 'Signal' Bookguide* (Thimble Press). A selection of some of the best poetry for children.

Brownjohn, Sandy (1980) *Does it Have to Rhyme?* and (1982) *What Rhymes with Secret?* (Hodder & Stoughton). Full of practical ideas for teaching poetry.

Brownjohn, Sandy and Whitaker, Janet (1985) *Word Games* and *Another Word Games* (Hodder Educational). Some practical ideas for playing with language, whilst introducing children to a number of poetic forms.

Chapple, S. (ed) (1989) *Becoming a Writer* (National Writing Project/Nelson). This book has some interesting ideas for using a writing environment to develop the young writer.

Corbett, Pie and Moses, Brian (1986) *Catapults and Kingfishers* (Oxford University Press). A range of good ideas for teaching poetry, fleshed out with children's work.

Edmonds, Jill and Williams, M. Carys (1985) *Storytime* (Chester College, Cheyney Road, Chester CH1 4BJ). This book discusses story forms, reading, writing and telling stories, with examples of children's work.

Graves, Donald (1983) *Writing: Teachers and Children at Work* (Heinemann Educational). Shows teachers helping children develop as writers, and deals with conferencing, classroom organisation, and talking to parents about writing.

Hall, Nigel (1989) *Writing with Reason* (Hodder & Stoughton). A useful book on the emergence of authorship.

Raban, Bridie (ed) (1985) *Practical Ways to Teach Writing* (Ward Lock Educational). Deals with the place of first-hand experience and structure in writing.

Rosen, Michael (1989) *Did I Hear You Write?* (Andre Deutsch). Attempts to get us to look at the ways we work with children in both written and spoken language.

Spelling

Bentley, Diana (1990) *Teaching Spelling* (Reading and Language Information Centre). Discusses the methods of teaching spelling, with an annotated list of recent spelling material.

Bentley, Diana and Karavis, Sylvia (1987) *Bright Ideas: Spelling* (Scholastic Publications). A collection of ideas for teaching spelling.

Cripps, Charles and Peters, Margaret L. (1980) *Catchwords: Ideas for Teaching Spelling* (Harcourt Brace Australia). This book outlines a systematic way of teaching spelling, with emphasis on the 'look, cover, visualise and write' technique.

Gentry, J. Richard (1987) *Spel... is a four-letter word* (Scholastic). A look at the assumptions behind the teaching of spelling.

Peters, Margaret Lee (1985) *Spelling: Caught or Taught?* (Routledge). Considers some different approaches to teaching spelling.

Todd, Joyce (1982) *Learning to Spell* (Basil Blackwell). Practical resources for teachers.

Torbe, Mike (1977) *Teaching Spelling* (Ward Lock Educational). Tries to answer some common questions about the teaching of spelling.

Handwriting

Droge, Dennis and Glander-Bandyk, Janice (1982) *An Introduction to Calligraphy* (David and Charles). Teaches the five basic styles of lettering, with detailed instructions for projects.

Jarman, Christopher *Helping Children With Their Writing* (Reading and Language Centre, Digby Stuart College, Roehampton Lane, London SW15 5PH). A useful guide.

Jarman, Christopher (1974) *Fun with Pens* (A&C Black). A brief history of writing, with ideas for presenting handwriting skills for young calligraphers.

Martin, Judy *The Complete Guide to Calligraphy* (Quill Publishing). A study of the development of writing, materials and basic letter forms.

Smith, Peter and Inglis, Alexander (1984); the *Nelson Handwriting* series.

Topic work

Hunt, Roderick (1984) *Ghosts, Witches and Things Like That* (Oxford University Press). A rich selection of ideas and activities.

Hurst, Keith, Aitken, Bob and Snow, Andrew (1985) *Witches, Halloween and Guy Fawkes* (Hodder & Stoughton). An excellent booklet from the very useful 'Beginnings' series.

Kerry, Trevor and Tollitt, Janice (1987) *Teaching Infants* (Basil Blackwell). Invites teachers to look at their practice and to explore it through task-related activities.

Roberts, S., Price, D. and Standing, G. (1987) *Birds and Beasts* (A. & C. Black). Songs, games and activities to develop and extend project work.

Assessment and record-keeping

Raban, Bridie (1983) *Guides to Assessment in Education: Reading* (Macmillan Educational). Looks at the various purposes of assessment, and discusses the underlying assumptions behind reading tests.

Southgate, V., Armold, H. and Johnson, S. (1981) *Extending Beginning Reading* (Heinemann Educational). This book, based on the Schools Council project of the same name, suggests ways in which children can be helped to become proficient and habitual readers.

Wilkinson, A., Davies, A. and Berrill, D. (1990) *Spoken English Illuminated* (Open University Press). A most illuminating book about children's talk and how to assess it.

Other resources

Books for Keeps (School Bookshop Association, 6 issues p.a.) has articles about children's books, and useful criticism *of the* current crop.

Creative Language (Stanley Thornes, 3 issues p.a.) is a photocopiable periodical with information and ideas on developing children's language.

LDA have equipment for all aspects of language teaching, from puzzles to tactile handwriting letter guides.

Photograph packs are available from Philip Green. Some of the packs have poems specially chosen for each picture.

The Practical Poetry Wordcard Pack by Paul Cleghorn can be very useful. It is available from Woodland Educational Press, 40 Hill Street, Alloa, Scotland.

Useful addresses

Children's Book Foundation,
Book Trust,
45 East Hill,
London SW18 2QZ

Philip Green Ltd,
112a Alcester Road,
Studley, Warks B80 7NR.

Hugglets Teddy Bear Magazine,
PO Box 290,
Brighton BN2 1DR

LDA,
Duke Street,
Wisbech, Cambs PE13 2AE.

The National Association for the Teaching of English (NATE),
Birley School Annexe,
Fox Lane Site,
Frecheville, Sheffield S12 4WY

National Oracy Project,
Newcombe House,
45 Notting Hill Gate,
London W11 3JB

National Writing Project,
c/o National Curriculum Council,
15-17 New Street,
York YO1 2RA

Reading and Language Information Centre,
University of Reading School of Education,
London Road,
Reading RG1 5AQ

Signal Book Guides,
Thimble Press,
Lockwood,
Station Road,
South Woodchester,
Stroud, Glos GL5 5QE

The United Kingdom Reading Association (UKRA),
c/o Edge Hill College of Further Education,
St Helen's Road,
Ormskirk, Lancashire.

A T CHART

Use this chart to identify the attainment targets which are covered by each of the activities in this book. The activities are numbered according to their place in the relevant chapter.

AT / CHAPTER	1 Speaking and listening	2 Reading	3 Writing	4 Spelling	5 Handwriting
1	1-22	12, 21, 23	15, 19, 21, 22		
2	1, 3, 4, 7, 9, 10, 17	1, 2, 4-8, 11-18	7, 8, 11	7, 8	8
3	19, 20, 21, 27, 31		1-31		9, 14
4		4, 5, 8, 9, 10, 12, 20, 23, 28	4, 5, 6, 7, 20	1-3, 6-9, 11-28	
5			1, 3, 4, 5	3, 4, 5, 6, 7, 11	1-12

PHOTOCOPIABLES

The pages in this section can be photocopied and adapted to suit your needs and those of your class; they do not need to be declared in respect of any photocopying licence.

Pages 154 to 174 each relate to a specific activitiy in the main body of the book. Pages 175 to 185 offer a range of formats to help with record-keeping and assessment. Pages 186 to 189 give a selection of useful word lists and finally pages 190 and 191 give line guides so that the children can place them under plain pieces of paper to keep their writing straight.

The appropriate activity and page references, where relevant, are given above each photocopiable sheet.

Find ☐ words about _ _ _ _ _ _ _ _ _ _
Make a list of them under the word-search grid.

My favourite programme is _ _ _ _ _ _ _ _
My favourite character is _ _ _ _ _ _ _ _
The best part is _ _ _ _ _ _ _ _

a b c d e
f g h i j
k l m n o

Reading record, page 34

Reading record for: _ _ _ _ _ _ _ _ _ _ _

Sheet number: _ _ _ _ _ _

Class: _ _ _ _

Date	Title	Page number	Who chose it?	Read to: self/ teacher/ parent	Own comments	Parent's/ teacher's comments

My diary, page 41

This is my diary for the week beginning Sunday _ _ _ _ _ _ _ _ _ _

| Sunday |
| Monday |
| Tuesday |
| Wednesday |
| Thursday |
| Friday |
| Saturday |

I liked _ best of all

because _

_ _

My favourite programme is _ _ _ _ _ _ _ _ _ _ _ _ _ _ _ _ _ _

My favourite character is _ _ _ _ _ _ _ _ _ _ _ _ _ _ _ _ _ _

The best part is when _ _ _ _ _ _ _ _ _ _ _ _ _ _ _ _ _ _

Other programmes I enjoy are

_ _

_ _

Write the answers to these questions and use them as the framework for your story.

Title of story

Who is in the story?

What are they going to do?

Where will they do it?

When will they do it?

Why will they do it?

How are they going to do it?

What will happen in the end?

100 common words, pages 60 and 62

100 common words – checklist

Pupil's name _ _ _ _ _ _ _ _ _ _ _

First 16

Word	Date started	Mastered	Checked
a			
he			
in			
it			
of			
the			
to			
went			

Word	Date started	Mastered	Checked
and			
I			
is			
my			
that			
then			
was			
with			

Next 24

am			
at			
for			
had			
have			
his			
me			
out			
see			
some			
they			
we			

are			
come			
go			
has			
her			
little			
one			
saw			
she			
there			
this			
when			

100 common words (continued)

Remaining 60 words

Word	Date started	Mastered	Checked
about			
all			
as			
back			
because			
but			
call			
can			
did			
down			
get			
here			
into			
like			
look			
make			
next			
now			
old			
once			
our			
put			
so			
their			
three			
today			
two			
up			
were			
will			

Word	Date started	Mastered	Checked
after			
an			
away			
be			
big			
by			
came			
could			
do			
from			
got			
him			
last			
live			
made			
new			
not			
off			
on			
other			
over			
said			
take			
them			
time			
too			
us			
very			
what			
you			

Write the word in the left panel.
Fold each panel underneath when you try again.

Word to learn	Try it here	and here	and here
Check ___	Check ___	Check ___	Check ___

Word to learn	Try it here	and here	and here
Check ___	Check ___	Check ___	Check ___

Write your name here — — — — — — — — — — — —

Join the letters in order.
Start at the letter a.

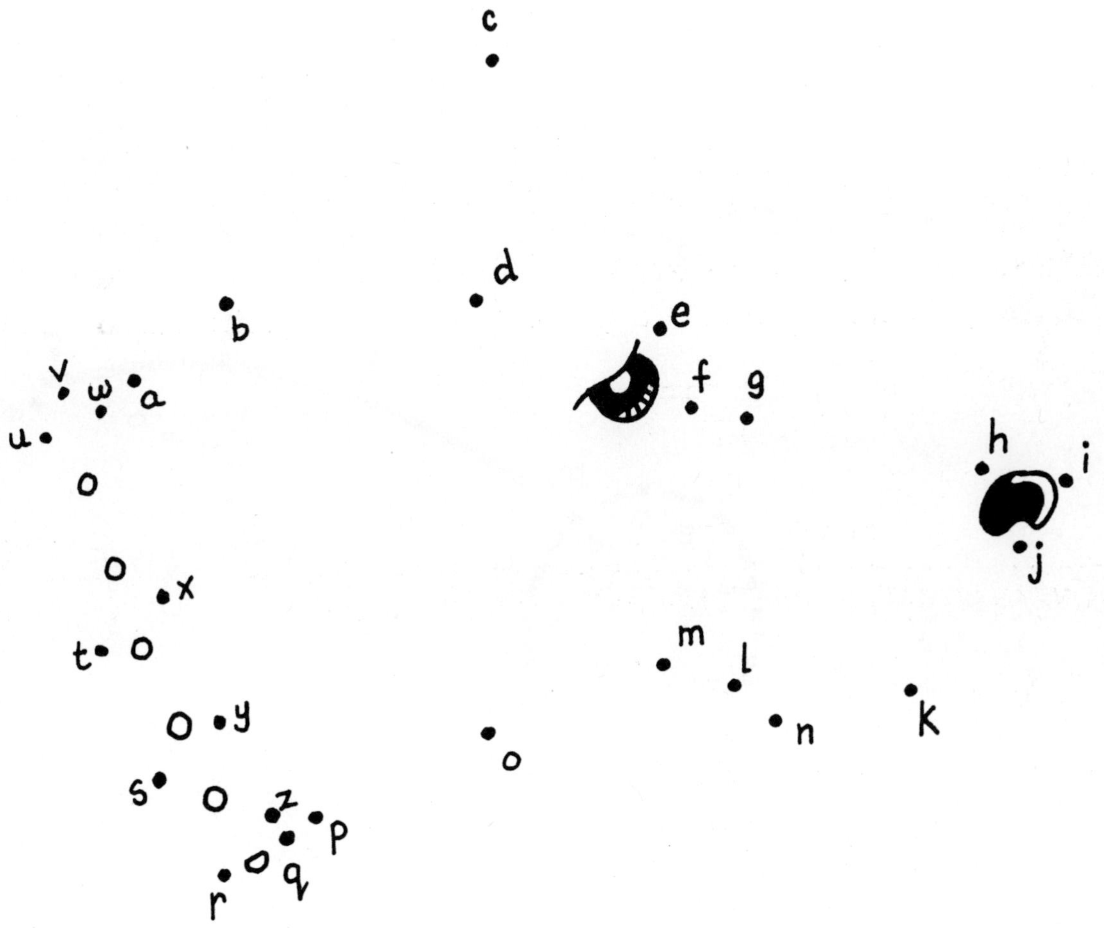

c
·

d
·

·b

e
·

f   g
·   ·

h
·   ·i

·a   j
·

u·

o

o   ·x

t· o

o ·y

s· o   m   l   k
·   ·   ·   ·
o   ·n
·z
· ·p
o
r· q

Write your name here —————————————

Join the letters in order.
Start at the letter a.

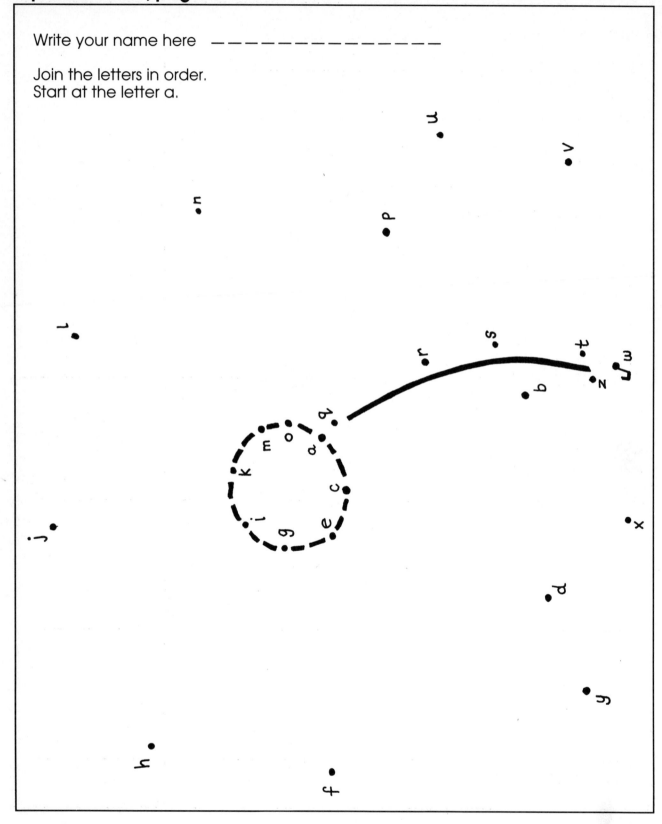

Word masters, page 68

Name _ _ _ _ _ _ _ _ _ _ _ _ _ _ _ _ _ _

Date _ _ _ _ _ _ _ _ _ _ _ _ _ _ _ _ _

Look at this word

Use it to make more words.

1   2   3   4

Use this letter group to complete these words:

Look for the words you have made and others like them in this word-search grid.

Put a line through the words you find and list them here.

Copy the circles on to
thin card, and fill in some
suffixes and prefixes as
shown below.

Then fasten the circles
together with a paper
fastener.

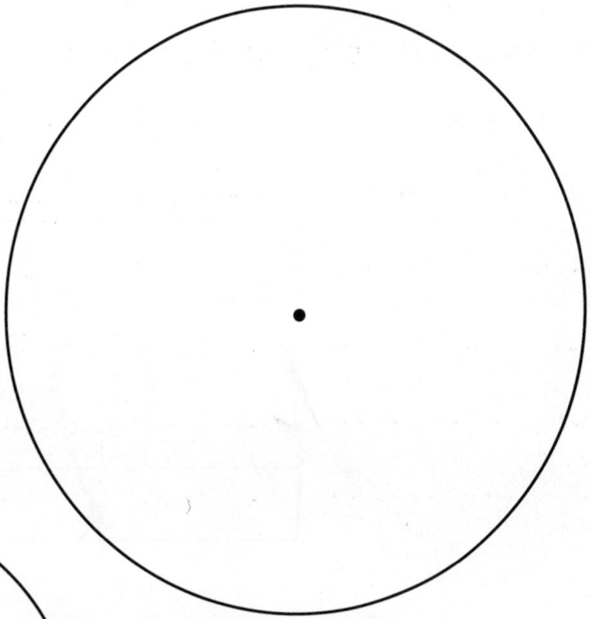

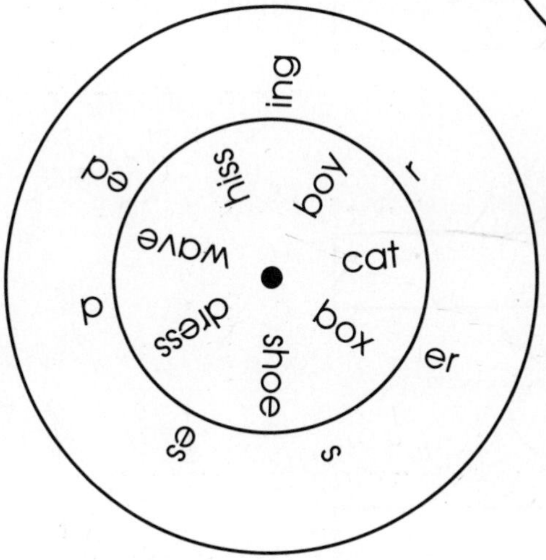

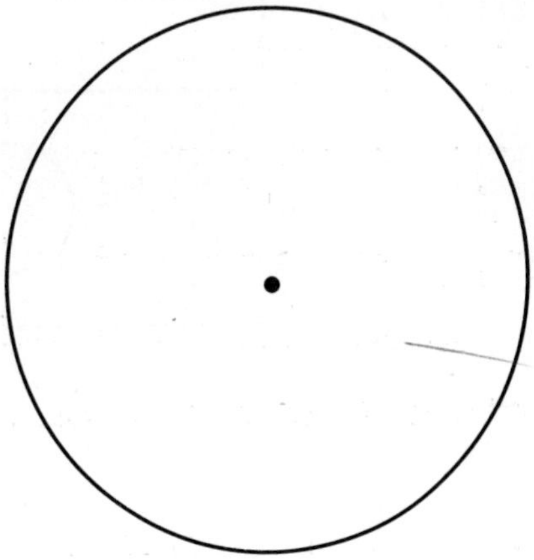

ing

ed
hiss
boy
r
wave
cat
d
dress
box
es
shoe
s
er

Plus or minus, page 74

Words with [ ] in them.

+ 1 in the circle means add one letter.
− 1 means take away one letter.
× 1 means change one letter.

Word-search, page 74

Find ☐ words about _ _ _ _ _ _ _ _ _ _ _ _ _ _

Make a list of them under the word-search grid.

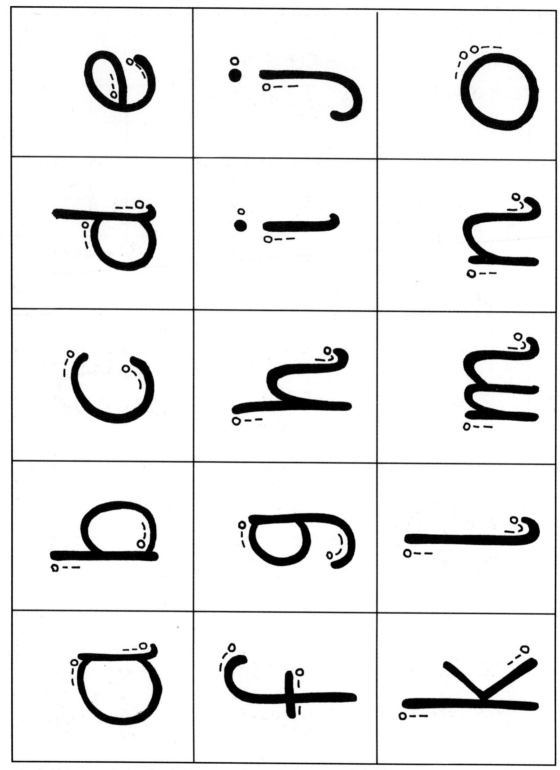

Colour the starting dots and dashes green and the finishing ones red.

t	y	
s	x	z
r	w	u
q	v	
p	w	N

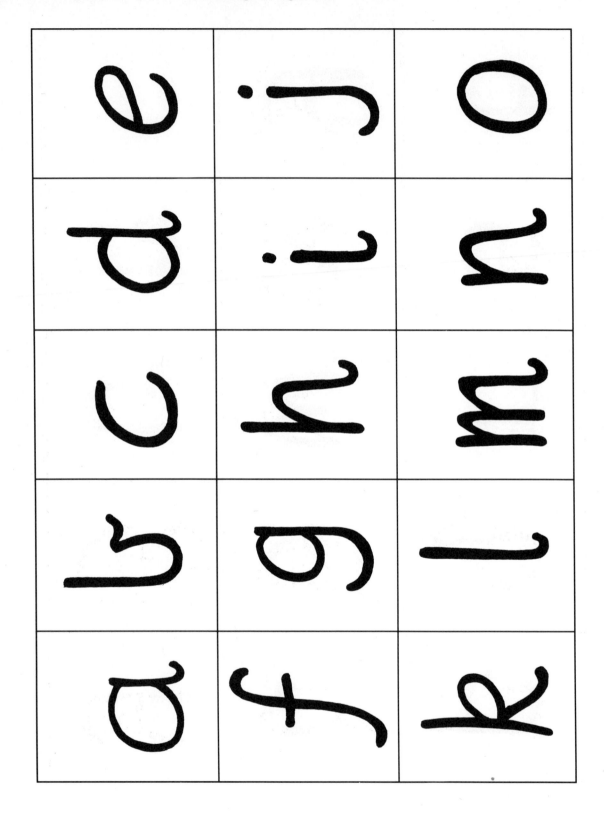

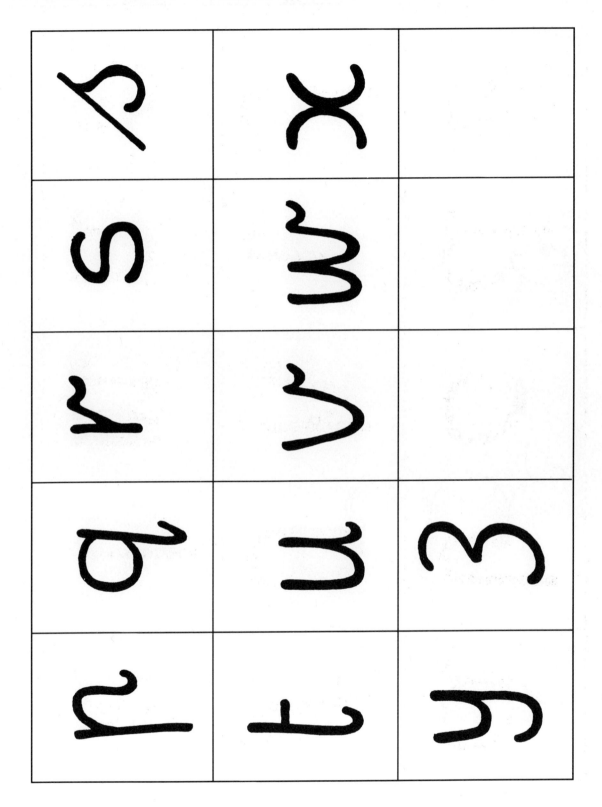

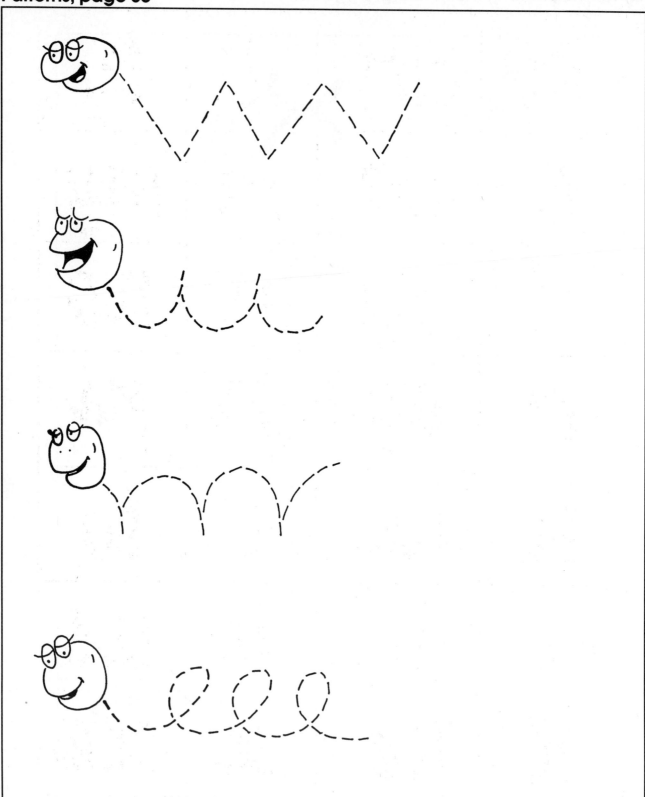

a	an	l	ly
c	co	m	my
d	da	n	no
e	ey	r	pi
h	hu	t	to
i	u	it	us
k	ke	x	xe

Horizontal joins with examples.

These letters do not join.

b	by	g	go
f	fo	j	ja
o	or	q	qu
r	ry	s	so
v	va	s	ss
w	we	3	3o

Topic theme recording chart

Topic theme: — — — — — —

Teacher's name: — — — — — —

	Autumn 1 2
	Spring 1 2
	Summer 1 2

English	Mathematics	Science	Geography	History
Speaking and listening				
Reading				
Writing	Design and technology	Art	Music	Religious education
Spelling				
Handwriting				

Use this card to check your writing, then bring it to me.

Read the first instruction. Do what it says. Now do the rest, one at a time.

1. Check to see that you have done what you were asked to do.

2. Read through your work and see if it makes sense.

3. Put in any words you have left out.

4. Cross out any words you do not need.

5. Put a wiggly line under words that may not be spelled correctly. Find the correct spelling in a dictionary. Correct your spelling.

6. Make sure there is a full stop at the end of each sentence. Make sure there is a question mark at the end of each question.

Now you are ready to come and talk to me about your writing.

Check your writing – 2

When you have finished getting your ideas down, you may need to move parts of your work around or change the way it is written. You may need to cut words out or put in extra ones to make your writing more interesting.

When you have worked on your writing, ask a friend to check it through with you.

These questions will help you look for important things in your writing.

1. Have you done what you were asked to do?

2. Does your writing say what you want it to say?

3. Is the meaning clear to others?

4. Is it in the right style?

5. Does the first paragraph make people want to read on?

6. Are the events in the right order?

7. Does it have a satisfactory ending?

8. Does your writing need descriptive words and images? If so, have you made good and proper use of them?

9. Have you left out anything important to your writing?

10. Are there any bits you could cut out to make your writing more interesting?

Good spelling and correct punctuation make our work easier for others to understand. We all make mistakes in our writing, from time to time, so it's a good idea to check work when we have finished to correct any mistakes that may be there.

Read these questions one at a time. Do what each one says before you go on to the next one. Ask a friend to check your work through with you and talk about any changes you need to make.

1. Have you put a clear title to your work?

2. Have you put a wiggly line under any word that could be wrong, and checked it in a dictionary?

3. Have you started a new sentence every time with each new thought or happening?

4. Do all the sentences begin with a capital letter and end with a full stop?

5. Does each question end with a question mark?

6. Have you put a speech mark at the beginning and end of someone speaking?

7. Have you started a new paragraph when someone else starts to speak?

8. Have you used commas to separate words in a list, or to mark off different parts of a sentence?

9. Have you written the date?

10. Is your name clearly written on the paper?

Recording chart for work in progress

Class _____ Subject _____ Term _____ Year _____

Title of task											
Type of task											
Date set											

Pupils' names

Use a key like this to keep track of work in progress: R = rough; D = in draft; F = finished; L = late

Assessment sheet

Topic theme	Aspects of writing covered								Spelling			Handwriting			
Child's name															

Key: N = not retained; B = beginning to grasp; K = knows and uses

Self-assessment in English

Name — — — — — — —   Class — — — — — — —   Date — — — — — — —

Use these questions to help you think about your English work,
then answer the questions honestly.

1. What have you enjoyed doing?

2. What do you think you did well?

3. Was there any work you disliked doing?

4. Tick the things you would like more help with:

☐   Reading

☐   Writing stories

☐   Writing poems

☐   Writing about real things

☐   Comprehension

Self-assessment in English (continued)

☐   Spelling

☐   Handwriting

☐   Making notes

☐   Information diagrams

☐   Full stops

☐   Using capital letters

☐   Finding things in the library

☐   Saying what you want to say in discussion

☐   Anything else? Write it here.

5. Which one would you like help with first?

6. How can you set about improving your work?

7. Write a short report about your English work – be honest!

8. Choose a piece of work that you are especially pleased with. Copy it out carefully and add it to this report.

Reading checklist

Name _ _ _ _ _ _ _ _   Class _ _ _ _ _ _   Date _ _ _ _ _ _ _

To be filled in by teacher and pupil together.

A. HOW DO YOU READ?

1. Do you read
   only at school/at home once a week/every day?

2. Have you always got your nose in a book,
   or do you never read from choice?

3. Do you read
   silently to yourself/saying words as you read/aloud in a group/
   aloud to an adult/all of these?

4. Do you borrow books from the school library or the public library
   regularly/occasionally/never?

B. WHAT DO YOU READ?

5. What is the story you have enjoyed most –
   reading to yourself?
   being read to you?

6. What are you reading at the moment –
   at home?
   at school?

7. What is being read to you at school at the moment?

C. READING ALOUD

Read aloud from a book of your choice to your teacher. After talking to you about your reading your teacher will write some comments which you may read.

8. Comments –

D. COMPREHENSION

The teacher will ask you some questions about your reading.

9. Can the pupil answer simple questions about the passage?

10. Can the pupil retell the story showing understanding and retention ofdetail?

11. Can the pupil predict what is likely to happen next?

12. Have there been any changes in the pupil's reading since last time?

Individual writing record

This record, filled in by the pupil, itemises the written work and the writing genres attempted as well as his/her attitude towards the tasks. Use half-termly or monthly and keep in the pupil's portfolio or record file.

Name _ _ _ _ _ _ _ _ _ _   **Class** _ _ _ _ _ _ _ _ _ _

List all the writing you have done this week and say what you thought about the tasks you were given.

Date	Writing task	Comments

Homophones

Select homophones from this list which relate to your topic
for games and activities.

air, heir	hear, here	rain, reign, rein
aloud, allowed	heard, herd	read, reed
alter, altar	hire, higher	right, write
arc, ark	hole, whole	ring, wring
bare, bear	hour, our	road, rode, rowed
beach, beech	key, quay	root, route
be, bee	knew, new	rose, rows
blue, blew	knight, night	sail, sale
bored, board	knot, not	scene, seen
bow, bough	knows, nose	seam, seem
boy, buoy	leak, leek	sew, so, sow
by, bye, buy	lightening, lightning	shore, sure
ceiling, sealing	made, maid	sight, site
cellar, seller	mail, male	soar, sore
cereal, serial	mare, mayor	sole, soul
check, cheque	meet, meat	son, sun
chute, shoot	medal, meddle	stair, stare
coarse, course	missed, mist	stake, steak
currant, current	more, moor	stationary, stationery
draft, draught	one, won	tail, tale
deer, dear	pail, pale	team, teem
ewe, yew, you	pain, pane	their, there
fair, fare	pause, paws	threw, through
feet, feat	peace, piece	tide, tied
flour, flower	peak, peek	to, too, two
foul, fowl	peal, peel	vain, vane, vein
groan, grown	peer, pier	waist, waste
hale, hail	plain, plane	weak, week
hair, hare	practice, practise	where, wear
hall, haul	principle, principal	wood, would

Plurals

Here are some common rules for the plural endings of words.

Words ending in -ay, -ey, -oy, -uy: add s

bay
castaway
day
holiday
jay
motorway
quay
ray
tray
way

abbey
alley
donkey
galley
jockey
journey
key
monkey
pulley
storey
trolley
valley

alloy
buoy

Words ending in -f and -fe

some change to -ves:

calf	shelf
elf	theif
half	wolf
loaf	
scarf	knife
self	life
sheaf	wife

some can end in either -ves or -s:

hoof
wharf

and some always end in -s:

bailiff	proof
chief	roof
cliff	reef
dwarf	safe
gulf	sheriff
handkerchief	waif
plaintiff	whiff

Words ending with -s, -ss, -x, -zz: add -es

atlas
gas

boss
class
compass
dress
duchess
glass
grass
hiss
hostess
kiss
lass
mass
miss
pass
princess
waitress

fax
tax
sex
fix
mix
box
fox
(exception: ox – oxen)

buzz

Words ending in -y: change to -ies

army	galaxy
baby	gipsy
battery	gooseberry
berry	hobby
body	lady
boundary	lily
brewery	lorry
bully	lottery
candy	lullaby
canary	melody
century	memory
cherry	pansy
city	poppy
comedy	quarry
dairy	raspberry
diary	ruby
dragonfly	spy
fairy	story
family	strawberry
filly	study
folly	sty

Words inside words

Choose words which are appropriate to current work; the list below gives some possible examples. Ask the children to find the words within words, keeping to the original letter order so that the pattern through the word is evident. For example:

amusement
am
  muse
    us
    use
       me
      men

another	grandfather	pitcher
credited	hippopotamus	postage
disappearance	interesting	shopping
discovered	kingfisher	teacher
everywhere	knowledge	thinking
father	listening	tomatoes
feather	missionary	unknown
fisherman	mother	withering
following	passing	

Line guides

Use these lines under plain paper to keep your writing straight.

Line guides

Use these lines under plain paper to keep your writing straight.